Shakespeare's Villains

Shakespeare's Villains

By
Maurice Charney

FAIRLEIGH DICKINSON UNIVERSITY PRESS
Madison, NJ

Published by Fairleigh Dickinson University Press
A wholly owned subsidary of The Rowman & Littlefield Publishing Group, Inc.
4501 Forbes Boulevard, Suite 200, Lanham, Maryland 20706
www.rowman.com

10 Thornbury Road, Plymouth PL6 7PP, United Kingdom

British Library Cataloguing in Publication Information Available

Library of Congress Cataloging-in-Publication Data

The hardback edition of this book was previously cataloged by the Library of Congress as
follows:

Charney, Maurice.
  Shakespeare's villains / by Maurice Charney.
      p. cm.
  Includes bibliographical data and index.
  1. Shakespeare, William, 1564-1616—Characters—Villains. 2. Villains in literature. I.
Title.
  PR2992.V5C46 2012
  822.3'3—dc23
                                                              2011043288

ISBN 978-1-61147-497-8 (cloth : alk. paper)
ISBN 978-1-61147-621-7 (pbk. : alk. paper)
ISBN 978-1-61147-498-5 (electronic)

Printed in the United States of America

In loving memory of
Hanna

Contents

Acknowledgments

Shakespeare is quoted from the individual volumes of *The Complete Signet Classic Shakespeare*, edited by Sylvan Barnet (New York: Harcourt Brace Jovanovich, 1972), except for *King Lear,* which is quoted from the Arden edition, 3rd series, ed. R.A. Foakes (London:Thomson Learning, 1997). I have made good use of the notes and introductions in the Arden editions and in the Signet. I have footnoted only special issues in an effort to avoid excessive footnoting, but I have profited greatly from conversation with my colleagues at Rutgers and with members of the Shakespeare Seminar at Columbia University.

I presented a paper on Tybalt at the Shakespeare Seminar. Since just about everyone disagreed that Tybalt was a villain, I took this as a strong sign of the intellectual vitality of that seminar. I also want to thank Angelika Zirker of the University of Tübingen for providing me with a preliminary bibliography on Shakespeare's villains. Maik Goth of Ruhr University at Bochum kindly lent me a copy of his original bok connecting Iago and Vice tradition

I have made abundant use of *The Harvard Concordance to Shakespeare*, ed. Marvin Spevack (Cambridge: Harvard University Press, 1973). I also refer frequently to the *Oxford English Dictionary*, abbreviated as the *OED*. The dates of Elizabethan and Jacobean plays are from Alfred Harbage, *Annals of English Drama 975–1700*, rev. S. Schoenbaum (London: Methuen, 1964). For proverbs, I refer to the numbering system in Morris Palmer Tilley, *A Dictionary of the Proverbs in England in the Sixteenth and Seventeenth Centuries* (Ann Arbor: University of Michigan Press, 1966).

Introduction

This book is about Shakespeare's villains, and calumniators and tyrants, too, as they are related to villains. When I first began this project, I was surprised that there was no single book on this subject, although a great deal has been written about individual characters. The topic is closely connected with an understanding of evil in Shakespeare. I think that readers and audiences alike are surprised at how important villains were to Shakespeare. In *Othello*, for example, the nefarious Iago almost steals the show from the rightful protagonist. Iago is clever, inventive, and subtle, a quick and ingenious improviser, not qualities that Othello is noted for. He is also very persuasive and an excellent actor who plays many parts and can speak in many different styles to accomplish his objectives. He is also wonderfully in touch with the audience and speaks many soliloquies to make sure that the audience is fully informed about what he is doing. Iago is a plotter like Shakespeare himself, who is writing this play. We will never know why Shakespeare was so skillful in his creation of villains, but the question is an intriguing one.

The question has a practical side to it because there are so many different kinds of villains (and calumniators and tyrants, too) in Shakespeare. This book is very much devoted to a close reading of the plays in order to find out how the villains operate and what their preoccupations are, in terms of their images, language, and overall styles. I have not spoken a great deal about the intricate body of ideas that lie behind the villains. I hope to bring readers of Shakespeare and people who go to see the plays into some realization of the crucial role that villains play, even minor villains like Tybalt, Iachimo, and Angelo. They establish an elaborate network of evil—what constitutes the world of the play—in which the good characters must function. I think we are rightfully stung by how easily villains like Iago can dupe their victims.

There is a kind of gleeful gloating in Iago as he triumphs over the honest and trusting Othello. This gloating is also present in Cassius as he discovers that Brutus can be won over to the conspiracy without much effort, by fair means or foul. Evil is rampant in Shakespeare, and the villains seem to be able to overpower the virtuous characters—at least for a time—because the virtuous characters, by their very nature, are so credulous, trusting, and unsuspecting, whereas the villains are always so extremely wary. Villains are generally subtle and ingenious, excellent role-players and actors. It is not surprising that Shakespeare should be so suspicious of actors and acting as creators of false appearances.

I would like to try to define some of the characteristics that many of the villains share. These are, of course, only tentative generalizations, since there are so many exceptions. One obvious point is that most of the villains are either murderers or capable of murder. I think what Shylock says in *The Merchant of Venice* is important here: "Hates any man the thing he would not kill?" (4.1.67). This question is unanswerable because there is no necessary link between hatred and killing, as Shylock seems to think. But among Shakespeare's villains there is an additional element of sport, as in Aaron, Richard (Duke of Gloucester and later King Richard III), Iago, and others, who think of killing as a kind of game, in which the main thing is to show how clever you are in outwitting your antagonist. Macbeth as a villain-hero is different, because he is so powerfully convinced of his own guilt in killing, but he kills nevertheless in his overweening ambition to be king. In this he is supported by his wife. Claudius, too, feels great guilt about his murders, but this feeling doesn't prevent him from annihilating his enemies (or his imagined enemies).

It is not surprising that many villains are creatures of will, as Iago pronounces so vigorously to Roderigo:

> Virtue? A fig! 'Tis in ourselves that we are thus, or thus. Our bodies are our gardens, to the which our wills are gardeners; so that if we will plant nettles or sow lettuce, set hyssop and weed up thyme, supply it with one gender of herbs or distract [vary] it with many . . . why, the power and corrigible authority of this lies in our wills. (*Othello* 1.3.314–21)

As creatures of will, villains pursue their ambitious projects with a cynical indifference to what anyone else thinks. They are fixated on themselves as the center of the universe. This is stated very simply in *Julius Caesar*. Caesar explains to Decius, a conspirator who is determined to bring him to the Capitol, why he cannot come: "The cause is in my will: I will not come" (2.2.71). It is not important that Calphurnia, Caesar's wife, has had ominous dreams, which Decius twists around with the promise of a crown for Caesar, who is finally persuaded to come—to be assassinated.

Shakespeare's villains are arbitrary and irrational in the pursuit of their wills, as if they need to consult with no one else among their many counselors. In his mad jealousy of his wife in *The Winter's Tale*, Leontes rejects all arguments to the contrary, even from those nearest and dearest to him. He is resolved to pursue his indomitable will even after the oracle at Delphi has declared against him, right up to the news that his dear son Mamillius is dead. Only this fact can persuade him to abandon his paranoid jealousy.

Linked with the villains as creatures of will is their lack of belief in anything greater than themselves. In religious terms, some of the villains are outright atheists, like Aaron in *Titus Andronicus* or even more obviously Edmund in *King Lear*. When he proclaims: "Thou, Nature, art my goddess; to thy laws/ My services are bound" (1.2.1–2), it is Nature red in tooth and claw, the law of the jungle, completely set apart from Christian revelation. In the same scene Edmund waxes satirical about his father's superstitious fears:

This is the excellent foppery of the world, that when we are sick in fortune, often the surfeits of our own behaviour, we make guilty of our disasters the sun, the moon and the stars, as if we were villains on necessity, fools by heavenly compulsion, knaves, thieves and treachers by spherical predominance; drunkards, liars and adulterers by enforced obedience of planetary influence; and all that we are evil in by a divine thrusting on. An admirable evasion of whoremaster man, to lay his goatish disposition on the charge of a star. (1.2.118–28)

To Edmund everything depends on the force of the individual will and on nothing else—certainly nothing metaphysical or religious.

Soliloquies and asides are very important to many of Shakespeare's villains, who want to be in close touch with the audience. The soliloquies are partly confessional and partly boastful, since the villains want to be considered absolutely honest with the spectators—"honest" is a much repeated word in *Othello* and *Julius Caesar*. Like Iago and Richard, Duke of Gloucester, villains wish to present themselves as plain and unadorned speakers (although they can also use slang and colloquial language when it suits their purpose). They seek not just the audience's approval but its sympathy and its praise. They take pride in their cleverness and in their superiority to ordinary mortals, and they show only contempt for the credulousness of their victims.

Many of Shakespeare's villains have a low opinion of women, if they are not overtly misogynistic. In Richard III's wooing of Anne, for example, he seduces her in a kind of game or sport, but after she has exited, he has only contempt for her. He mocks her in his soliloquy:

Was ever woman in this humor wooed?
Was ever woman in this humor won?
I'll have her, but I will not keep her long. (1.2.117–19)

Anne's early death is already predicted—she will be murdered by Richard.

In *Othello* Iago eggs Roderigo on by provocative enticements about Desdemona's torrid sexual needs:

When the blood is made dull with the act of sport, there should be a game to
inflame it and to give satiety a fresh appetite, loveliness in favor, sympathy in
years, manners, and beauties; all of which the Moor is defective in.
(2.1.225–29)

In Renaissance physiology, the blood was thought to be the seat of sexual
appetite. Iago says all this even though he knows that his slandering of
Desdemona as a whorish creature is a product of his own imagination and
that she remains, in his own words, "All guiltless" (4.1.49). Like many of
Shakespeare's villains, Iago's talk is very sexual, although he doesn't seem
to have any concept of love.

Villains in Shakespearean tragedy are essential to his presentation of tragic
themes, and this is also true of his history plays, many of which are tragic
in feeling. But the villains (and calumniators and tyrants) in his comedies
pose special problems. This is nowhere more obvious than in the actions
of Don John in *Much Ado About Nothing*. His calumniation of Hero, which
results in her supposed death, is weakly motivated and seems anomalous in
this play. Don John seems to be playing out his own vengeful and unsub-
stantiated impulses, as if something dire is needed to cure his melancholy.
This work discusses a number of villains, calumniators, and tyrants from
the comedies—Shylock, Angelo, Don John, Iachimo, Lucio, Leontes, and
Duke Frederick—most of whom are substantially affected by the fact that
they appear in comedies. The happy ending, for example, in comedies and
tragicomedies alters the direction the characters seem to be moving earlier
in their plays. In many comedies villainous figures serve as blocking agents
to prevent the course of true love from running too smoothly. They provide
necessary perturbations for the comic action. I have, however, omitted most
of them from the discussion. Undoubtedly, characters such as Sebastian
and Antonio (and Caliban too) from *The Tempst* and Cloten and his Queen
Mother from *Cymbeline* have a function similar to Don John's in *Much Ado
About Nothing*.

The word "villain" (and related forms) is extremely common in Shakespeare, as seen in Hamlet's exclamation about Claudius right after he has
spoken with his father's Ghost: "O villain, villain, smiling, damnèd villain"

(1.5.106). But the word has less force than it does now, because "villain" in its etymological (French) sense also refers to a peasant or servant or any base person. The *Oxford English Dictionary* defines "villain" in its double sense as "1. Originally, a low-born base-minded rustic; a man of ignoble ideas or instincts; in later use, an unprincipled or depraved scoundrel; a man naturally disposed to base or criminal actions, or deeply involved in the commission of disgraceful crimes." The first recorded use of the word is in 1303.

There is a good example of the doubleness of this word in *Titus Andronicus*, when Chiron and Demetrius discover that their mother has given birth to a black baby:

> *Demetrius.* Villain, what hast thou done?
> *Aaron.* That which thou canst not undo.
> *Chiron.* Thou hast undone our mother.
> *Aaron.* Villain, I have done thy mother. (4.2.73–76)

Aaron is the mentor of Chiron and Demetrius, so that "villain" in this context is not a very strong word.

Much has been written about Shakespeare's villains, but everyone owes a large debt to A. C. Bradley's magisterial study, *Shakespearean Tragedy: Lectures on Hamlet, Othello, King Lear, Macbeth*, first published in 1904. Bradley considered the moral and ethical dimension of Shakespeare's characters with high seriousness. I am also much indebted to Bernard Spevack's work *Shakespeare and the Allegory of Evil: The History of a Metaphor in Relation to his Major Villains* (Columbia University Press, 1958). Spevack does a remarkable job of relating Shakespeare's villains, especially Iago, Aaron, Richard III, and Don John, to the Vice figure of English morality plays of the fifteenth century. He puts special emphasis on the histrionic quality of the Vice and his jocularity. This is a very original insight. Villains like Iago luxuriate in their own cleverness, and they understand their evil machinations as game or sport. Like the Vice, the villains are gleeful. That is why most of Shakespeare's villains (with the notable exception of Macbeth, who is a villain-hero) are not tragic. They are comic because they don't think of themselves as wrong-doers. This statement needs to be qualified by the remorse or compassion many villains show at the end of their plays, the sudden upwelling of conscience. Even Edmund in *King Lear* says: "Some good I mean to do,/ Despite of mine own nature" (5.3.241–42).

I have benefitted significantly from previous close readings of Shakespeare.Robert B. Heilman's *Magic in the Web: Action and Language in Othello* (Lexington, Kentucky: University of Kentucky Press, 1956) is a model of a careful, closely reasoned account of the play, especially of Iago.

Heilman makes excellent use of imagery and image patterns. I have also found Heilman's *This Great Stage: Image and Structure in King Lear* (Baton Rouge: University of Louisiana Press, 1948) very instructive for understanding Edmund, Goneril, Regan, and Cornwall. Wolfgang Clemen's close reading of *Richard III, A Commentary on Shakespeare's Richard III* (London: 1968, but first published in German in 1957) has also been a valuable resource. Among books important to my study, I want also to include the analyses of dramatic form by Marvin Rosenberg, notably *The Masks of Othello* (Berkeley: University of California Press, 1961) and *The Masks of King Lear* (Berkeley: University of California Press, 1972). By presenting opposing opinions about a scene or about how a line was spoken, they are subtly helpful in constructing an argument.

I begin the book with Iago, since he is clearly Shakespeare's most significant villain. His dramatic character is already anticipated by Aaron in *Titus Andronicus* and by Richard, Duke of Gloucester, who becomes King Richard III. Iago is extraordinary for his inventiveness and creativity. His plotting depends on improvisation, as if it is all very easy and spontaneous. For example, the handkerchief that Emilia finds suddenly falls into Iago's hands and becomes amazingly successful in deceiving Othello. But we are sure that Iago really doesn't need the handkerchief. Without much effort he could win Othello over with something else. Like many of Shakespeare's villains, Iago has abundant soliloquies. These put him in close contact with the audience, which is kept informed of his every move. It is important to him for the audience to like him and to sympathize with him. He doesn't consider himself a villain, but rather a very clever manipulator who has many different reasons for his actions. He is a skillful actor who can play many parts, and he always expresses a kind of glee for his bravura performances. This is very like the laughing Aaron in *Titus Andronicus.*

Tarquin in *The Rape of Lucrece* and Aaron in *Titus Andronicus* are Shakespeare's first villains, from early works dating from around 1594, but it is noteworthy how strongly they set the pattern for future villains. Both Tarquin and Aaron are creatures of powerful will, and both have remarkably little concern for the natural rights of other people. Tarquin is surprisingly moralistic, because he is certain that what he is doing is wrong and will have dire consequences. But he pursues the rape of Lucrece relentlessly, and he uses an abundant martial imagery. Both Aaron and Tarquin are very purposive, but they are also inventive and improvisational. Aaron is distinctively a laughing villain, like the Vice in the morality plays. He is redeemed from absolute villainy by his love for his black baby, but he also expresses a strong atheism. Like Edmund in *King Lear,* he believes only in Nature. Aaron resembles Democritus, the laughing philosopher, because he is cynically amused by his evil deeds and by the stupidity and gullibility of his fellow humans. Finally, both Tarquin and Aaron are ready to rape or kill to accomplish their ends.

Richard, Duke of Gloucester (who becomes King Richard III), is endlessly creative in his villainy. He pursues the crown, and despite many obstacles, he manages to kill everyone in his way. His physical deformity is closely associated with his villainy, but he woos and wins Anne as if he were a beautiful young lover. His own mother curses him. Richard is artful in killing off his enemies, and we are made to admire his histrionic skill. He is gleeful at how easy it is to manipulate appearances and how foolishly credulous everyone is. Like Iago after him, Richard is closely in touch with the audience, in whom he confides in his soliloquies. He needs the audience to admire him and to be astounded by his consummate plotting. Like a skillful actor, he can play many roles. At the end of *Richard III*, Richard is despondent as the ghosts of the many persons he has killed come to remind him of his villainy.

Although he appears in a comedy, Shylock is clearly a villain because, once the due date is past, he refuses the money many times over that he has lent Antonio and insists on taking the pound of flesh that is stipulated in his "merry" bond. He is a very purposive and determined character, and it is evident that he intends to kill Antonio right before our eyes. The flight of his daughter Jessica, who has stolen his money and jewels, to marry the Christian Lorenzo infuriates him. It is interesting that in *The Merchant of Venice* Shakespeare goes out of his way to give Shylock some justification for his hatred of Antonio, who expresses a gross anti-Semitism. Shylock has an extremely sympathetic (and much quoted) speech about the common humanity that Jews share with Christians: "Hath not a Jew eyes?" (3.1.55ff.), but we should remember that the speech ends with a call for vengeance. He is a curious, if not bizarre, figure in this play, but he relentlessly pursues the life of Antonio as if this were a tragedy of revenge and not a comedy.

In *Hamlet*, Claudius is a politic murderer who has killed his brother and usurped the throne of Denmark. He is noted in the play for his secrecy as well as his subtlety. Among his many homicidal actions, he sends Hamlet to be murdered in England; he doesn't make much effort to stop his Queen, Gertrude, from drinking the poisoned chalice; and he is responsible for the deaths of Laertes and of Rosencrantz and Guildenstern. Claudius has an important soliloquy in the middle of the play in which he acknowledges his guilt, like Cain who did the first murder, although he is also aware that his prayer is useless, since he is not penitent. He is abetted by his chief counselor, Polonius, who is not directly a villain but proceeds by "policy," a word very much linked with villains.

Macbeth is a villain-hero, an unusual role in Shakespeare. Even while he is committing murder, he is tormented by his own guilt. This presents us with a double perspective, because Macbeth is not only a brutal murderer but also a conscience-stricken soul in spiritual torment. The first step in his ambitious pursuit of the crown is to kill King Duncan, but further murders are necessary, so that Banquo and then Macduff's wife and children are hunted down. As the play proceeds, Macbeth becomes progressively less sensitive, ending in a despairing apathy. A great deal of emphasis is placed on the inability of both him and Lady Macbeth to sleep. She does not directly persuade her husband to commit murder, but she engages in an elaborate psychological process of unsexing, so that she can become a female warrior. The play ends with her madness and intense guilt. The play is very much preoccupied with gender issues, especially what it means to be a man, defined by military might.

King Lear has an abundance of evil-doers. Edmund, the bastard son of Gloucester, is a free spirit who believes only in the workings of Nature, like Iago and Aaron. He is a strong and determined villain, and from his atheism comes a total disregard for the lives and feelings of others; he is unconstrained by any moral imperatives. Lear's elder daughters, Goneril and Regan, are savage in their conspiracy against their aging father. When they shut their doors on Lear in the midst of a ferocious storm, they clearly don't care whether he lives or dies. Regan abets her husband Cornwall in the blinding of Gloucester, perhaps the cruelest scene in all of Shakespeare. Goneril and Regan both kill themselves for the love of Edmund, who doesn't plan to marry either of them. The evil deeds in this play penetrate to the very heart of a grim and uncompromising reality.

In *Measure for Measure*, the strict Angelo is promoted to be Duke of Vienna when Duke Vincentio withdraws, but he seems to be testing Angelo right from the beginning of the play. When Angelo first appears, he is represented as being extremely virtuous and cold, but he is soon tempted by Isabella, the novice of St. Clare and sister of Claudio, who is condemned to death for fornication. Angelo is very soon proposing that he will spare the life of Claudio if Isabella has an assignation with him. Angelo, of course, is determined that Claudio be executed. This is at the heart of his villainy. As is fitting for a tragicomedy, the Duke in *Measure for Measure* arranges things so that Claudio is never really put to death and that Mariana, to whom Angelo was once betrothed, is substituted for Isabella in the Duke's "bed trick." The play ends not with "measure for measure," as we might expect, but with everyone pardoned, including Angelo and Lucio.

Tybalt in *Romeo and Juliet* is not a major character, but he is a caricatural villain who speaks in the language of the Italian dueling manuals that were so popular at this time. He is an affected, somewhat ridiculous figure, whom his uncle, Lord Capulet, calls a "princox." Mercutio speaks satirically of him as the Prince of Cats. Tybalt is deeply committed to the feud between the Montagues and the Capulets at the very moment when it seems to be dying down. His killing of Mercutio precipitates the tragic action. He returns intending to kill Romeo, but Romeo kills him.

Chapter 10 is devoted to calumniators, who are not exactly villains but share many of their qualities. We deal with Don John in *Much Ado About Nothing*, Iachimo in *Cymbeline*, and Lucio in *Measure for Measure,* none of whom is a major character. Don John is an anomalous figure whose impulse to do evil is unexplained, so in that way he resembles the villains in the tragedies. He slanders Hero and breaks up her marriage to Claudio. Iachimo is more fully developed as an Italianate villain, whose cleverness overcomes the innocent Posthumus in his ill-fated bet on Imogen's virtue. He resembles Iago not only in name, but also in subtlety. Lucio is hardly a villain at all, but he is a satirical malcontent who vilifies the Duke and everyone he comes in contact with. But there is an underlying idea that he sometimes speaks the bitter truth, like Thersites in *Troilus and Cressida* and Apemantus in *Timon of Athens.* The fact that the calumniators are all figures in Shakespeare's comedies somewhat mollifies their evil intents, which tend to disappear by the time of the happy ending.

The final chapter is devoted to tyrants, who resemble villains in many ways, especially in their reliance on strong will. King Richard III and Macbeth are tyrants whom we have spoken about earlier. Another example is Julius Caesar, who speaks in the vaunting language of Shakespeare's villains; his death brings on a bloody civil war. In the first part of *The Winter's Tale*, Leontes's jealous rage brings about the deaths of his son Mamillius and his counselor Antigonus, as well as the supposed deaths of Hermione and her daughter. But the play is a tragicomedy, and his rage ends as suddenly as it began. In *As You Like It*, Duke Frederick has usurped the kingdom from his brother, Duke Senior. Oliver parallels the Duke in his oppression of his younger brother, Orlando. Both Duke Frederick and Oliver talk of killing their enemies, but in the comic world of the play this never happens.

Chapter 1

Iago

Iago is Shakespeare's archetypal villain,[1] who defines the parameters of what it means to be a villain. I'd like to start with him and then move on to other related figures. By the time that Shakespeare wrote *Othello*, probably around 1603 or 1604, he had already created significant villains such as Aaron in *Titus Andronicus,* Richard, Duke of Gloucester in *3 Henry VI* and *Richard III*, Shylock in *The Merchant of Venice*, and Claudius in *Hamlet*. Iago is not quite the same as these figures, but he sums up a whole series of characteristic traits and attitudes.

The first point to consider is Iago's absolute contempt for Roderigo, which echoes Sir Toby's relation with Sir Andrew in *Twelfth Night*. We hear again Sir Toby's constant reminder "Thou hadst need send for more money" (2.4.182–83) in Iago's repeated refrain: "Put money in thy purse" (1.3.335), which occurs four more times in this same speech and is echoed in the first line of Iago's soliloquy: "Thus do I ever make my fool my purse" (374). Iago wants to be sure that the audience knows that Roderigo is not his friend and that his supposed support of Roderigo's wooing of Desdemona is done solely for monetary gain. Iago is eager to convince the audience of his absolute contempt for Roderigo and of his own superiority to such a fool:

> For I mine own gained knowledge should profane
> If I would time expend with such snipe
> But for my sport and profit. (375–77)

"Snipe" (either in the singular or the plural) are foolish birds easily caught, which, like the woodcock, Shakespeare uses frequently to express contempt. Part of Iago's disdain for everyone, especially his enemies, comes from his feeling of great superiority.

1

Notice that he is duping Roderigo not only for his "profit" but also for his "sport." This is an expression of Iago the hunter, who enjoys tricking his antagonists for the sheer pleasure of the game. "Sport" bears significantly on Iago's motives, since it implies that he enjoys his plots for their own sake and not for any ulterior purpose they may serve. "Sport" offers a way of understanding Coleridge's otherwise puzzling account of Iago's "motive-hunting of motiveless malignity."[2] This use of "sport" implies that the villain, in this case Iago, delights in his own sense of triumph. The word "sport" celebrates the villain's creative energies, much like that of the playwright in writing his play.

There is a similar feeling in Act V in Iago's plot to use Roderigo to kill Cassio. Iago uses a slangy term to express his utter contempt for Roderigo: "I have rubbed this young quat almost to the sense,/And he grows angry" (5.1.11–12). This is the only use of "quat" in Shakespeare, and it refers to a pimple, a pustule, or small boil. Rubbing to the "sense" is a painful image of rubbing something raw. Iago has only disdain for Roderigo and for Cassio too:

> Now, whether he kill Cassio,
> Or Cassio him, or each do kill the other,
> Every way makes my gain. Live Roderigo,
> He calls me to a restitution large
> Of gold and jewels that I bobbed [stole] from him
> As gifts to Desdemona.
> It must not be. (12–18)

Iago is ruthless and sociopathic in his utter disregard for human life. Like most of Shakespeare's villains, he is a killer and only interested in his own success—his "gain"—even if it involves the deaths of Roderigo and Cassio. Iago finishes by stabbing Roderigo, who calls him "damned Iago! O inhuman dog!" (62). This is Shakespeare's familiar negative image for dogs.[3]

Iago expresses his contempt for Cassio very early in the play. Othello has passed him over for promotion in favor of Cassio, a bookish man unschooled in the practice of war:

> And what was he?
> Forsooth, a great arithmetician,
> One Michael Cassio, a Florentine,
> (A fellow almost damned in a fair wife)
> That never set a squadron in the field,
> Nor the division of a battle knows
> More than a spinster; unless the bookish theoric,

Wherein the tonguèd consuls can propose
As masterly as he. Mere prattle without practice
Is all his soldiership. (1.1.15–24)

Other than what he says himself, we never have any basis for thinking of Iago as an excellent soldier, well schooled on the battlefield. Again, we should note that he downgrades Cassio because he is a Florentine and not a Venetian, in the same way that Iago thinks that Othello is not really a Venetian but "an extravagant and wheeling stranger/ Of here and everywhere" (133–34).

Iago accuses Cassio of having sex with his wife, as if *Othello* were a revenge play and Iago were getting even with his enemies. But *Othello* is emphatically not a revenge play, or only a mock revenge play, and Iago is only fantasizing about a whole string of possibilities that are never developed in the play. We know, of course, that neither Othello not Cassio is cuckolding Iago, but Iago's mind runs idly on this conjecture:

I'll have our Michael Cassio on the hip,
Abuse him to the Moor in the right garb
(For I fear Cassio with my nightcap too). . . . (2.1.306–8)

Cassio is totally unaware of Iago's machinations, even after he has made Cassio drunk and Othello has dismissed him as his lieutenant. Afterward, when Cassio engages Iago to help him recover his lieutenancy, upon leaving Cassio praises Iago's honesty: "I never knew/A Florentine more kind and honest" (3.1.38–39). In other words, Cassio, who is a Florentine and not a Venetian, does not believe that even a Florentine could be more kind and honest than Iago. We are getting caught up in the tragic irony of the play.

One of the most revealing indications of Iago's diabolical impulses occurs in Act V, scene i in his plot against Cassio. His life is of no importance to Iago, but there is another underlying motive:

If Cassio do remain,
He hath a daily beauty in his life
That makes me ugly. . . . (18–20)

This is startling. What is there in Cassio's daily beauty that could make Iago ugly? "Daily beauty" in this context presumably indicates a beauty that a person possesses every day in daily life. It is something that someone has without any conscious effort. Obviously, Iago is aware that he doesn't possess any daily beauty in his life, which immediately makes him alert to his own ugliness. This shows him at his most poisonously envious, but it also uncovers an insight into his own diabolic nature, which is like that of Milton's Satan

observing Eve in the Garden of Eden in *Paradise Lost*. The daily beauty of
Cassio's life has never been remarked on by anyone else in the play, not even
by Bianca. It seems as if Iago, in order to be superior, needs to destroy everyone in the world besides himself, especially Cassio and his daily beauty.

Iago's contempt for Roderigo and Cassio offers us a way of understanding
his even greater hatred for Othello, which he begins to show in his second
speech in the play. Iago is enraged that the "Three great ones of the city"
who sued to Othello on his behalf are put off. Othello "Evades them with a
bombast circumstance,/Horribly stuffed with epithets of war" (1.1.12–13).
It is interesting how immediately Iago situates his conflict with Othello in
terms of style (which we shall discuss more fully at the end of this chapter).
He prides himself on being a plain speaker, a soldier, but of course this is
manipulative and hypocritical, since Iago can use so many different styles
that suit his nefarious purposes. Othello more honestly makes the soldier's
claim of being a plain speaker, as he tells the Venetian Senators: "Rude am I
in my speech,/And little blessed with the soft phrase of peace" (1.3.81–82).
Iago accuses Othello of a bombastic style—bombast was the cotton stuffing
used to pad out a jacket—full of circumlocution ("circumstance"); in other
words, an oratorical style. Othello does speak very grandly in the play before
he is overcome with jealousy, but then he switches to Iago's more curt style.
That is one of the shifts that marks the success of Iago's seduction.

Iago is explicit about his relation to Othello. He hates him but will proceed
by seeming friendliness: "I follow him to serve my turn upon him" (1.1.39).
"Turn" is a word with erotic overtones, as is all of Iago's discourse. The
jealous Othello says of Desdemona to Lodovico: "Sir, she can turn, and turn,
and yet go on/And turn again" (4.1.253–54). Iago is very direct in his attack
on Othello, and his contempt is obvious: "Were I the Moor, I would not be
Iago./In following him, I follow but myself" (1.1.54–55). In other words,
if the tables were turned and Iago were Othello, he would not be as easily
twisted as Othello is about to be. This is a point much repeated in the play.
Iago is eager to assert his own mastery. His false seeming will provide an
impenetrable disguise: "But I will wear my heart upon my sleeve/For daws
to peck at; I am not what I am" (61–62). Of course, we never find out what
Iago is really like. His interiority disappears, and Othello's final question will
remain forever unanswered: "Will you, I pray, demand that demi-devil/Why
he hath thus ensnared my soul and body?" (5.2.297–98). But Iago remains a
blank: "From this time forth I never will speak word" (300).

By the third scene of Act I, Iago is already developing his revenge plot
against Othello. Again we have Iago's characteristic word, "sport," as he
tells Roderigo: "If thou canst cuckold him, thou dost thyself a pleasure, me a
sport" (364–65). So Iago's imagined revenge is tinged with the idea that it is

merely "sport," or amusement.[4] The love match between Othello and Desdemona is reduced to "a frail vow betwixt an erring barbarian and supersubtle Venetian" (351–52). Iago hates the Moor, as he says several times, but he embroiders his account with a wandering fantasy of cuckoldry:

> it is thought abroad that 'twixt my sheets
> H'as done my office. I know not if't be true,
> But I, for mere suspicion in that kind,
> Will do, as if for surety. (378–81)

Iago seems to be intent on making it seem as if he taking a just revenge on Othello, although he also knows that he is making it all up as he goes along.

The most disturbing aspect of Iago's plan—but to call it a plan is not quite right since it is all invented on the spot—is how much contempt he feels for his victims because they are so gullible. Of course, they are so credulous because they are so honest and virtuous. We feel Iago gloating when he observes:

> The Moor is of a free and open nature
> That thinks men honest that but seem to be so;
> And will as tenderly be led by th' nose
> As asses are. (390–93)

Othello is so vulnerable because he is "of a free and open nature," all the things that Iago is not—he prides himself on his wariness and his subtlety. He is always on his guard and untrusting, which is why he considers himself much shrewder than his opponents. Othello's trusting nature leads to his undoing, but this is also true of Roderigo, Cassio, Desdemona, Emilia, and probably all the other characters in the play. Iago is almost officially sealed as "honest Iago," an adjective that is repeated almost a dozen times without any irony, except for the audience.[5]

Iago speaks of Desdemona in much the same way that he does of Othello, and here we see the villain as a self-conscious plotter:

> So will I turn her virtue into pitch,
> And out of her own goodness make the net
> That shall enmesh them all. (2.3.360–62)

Iago is such a successfully conceived villain that it is necessary to insist that Desdemona is totally virtuous and not even partially responsible for her own fate. Students are so imbued with the belief that "where there's smoke, there's fire" that one has to dwell on passages like the one above, where Iago tells us that he is inventing the whole plot from scratch.

We should pause for a moment to look at some other plays before *Othello* in which there is a similar kind of disturbing gloating. Cassius in *Julius Caesar* is hardly a villain like Iago, but nevertheless he is excessively proud of the way he will trick Brutus into joining the conspiracy. In his scene-ending soliloquy, Cassius, like Iago, takes pleasure in his persuasive skills, which can work only because Brutus is so honest:

Well, Brutus, thou art noble; yet I see
Thy honorable mettle may be wrought
From that it is disposed; therefore it is meet
That noble minds keep ever with their likes;
For who so firm that cannot be seduced? (1.2.308–12)

In other words, Cassius is deliberately excluding himself from being a noble mind and of honorable mettle like Brutus. Brutus and Othello are easily seduced by persons who are not as trusting and as credulous as they are. Cassius echoes the words that Iago speaks later when he says: "If I were Brutus now, and he were Cassius,/He should not humor me" (314–15). Cassius is very proud of his cleverness and his trickery. He is not an "ass" who can be led by the nose as Othello is by Iago.

Prince Hal in the *Henry IV* plays is also not a villain, yet he shares some of Iago's disturbing gloating. In both Iago and Cassius, gloating is an expression of superiority. I find a similar attitude in Hal's sharp separation of himself from his boon companions in Eastcheap. His scene-ending soliloquy early in *1 Henry IV* is chilling: "I know you all, and will awhile uphold/ The unyoked humor of your idleness" (1.2.199–200). He is already anticipating his reformation, "Redeeming time when men think least I will" (221). This is disturbing because Hal is temporizing with his merry companions. There is a clear line between this soliloquy—Hal's "I do, I will" (2.4.481) at the end of the scene in which Hal and Falstaff act each other's roles—and Hal's rejection of Falstaff in *2 Henry IV* (5.5.48ff.). All of these speeches claim that Falstaff and his companions are merely a fantasy or bad dream. Now that Hal has awakened from his dream and returned to real life, he can easily say: "I have long dreamt of such a kind of man" (50). The three speeches connect in their crassness. Hal is deliberate and superior like Iago and Cassius. He is hardly "of a free and open nature" like Othello.

Let us return to Iago. He is a plotter, and like Shakespeare himself, he is busy writing his own play that will precipitate Othello's downfall,[6] an event that brings with it not only Othello's death, but the deaths of Desdemona,

Emilia, and Roderigo. By way of putting him off, Iago tells Roderigo: "Thou know'st we work by wit, and not by witchcraft;/ And wit depends on dilatory time" (2.3.373–74). "Wit" is a complex word in Shakespeare that goes beyond witty remarks in conversation. It means something like what we would call intelligence in modern English, with the additional idea that a witty person has a strong imagination or powers of invention. Thus Richard III rejects "The deep-revolving witty Buckingham" (*Richard III* 4.2.42), who hesitates to agree to the murder of the princes in the Tower. Iago is a plotter, but in the wit and witchcraft passage "wit" indicates what Iago is best at: quick, spontaneous bursts of ideas. Iago is throughout a brilliant improviser rather than a deeply considered plotter.[7]

This is obvious in Iago's soliloquy at the end of Act I, scene iii. He hits upon the scheme that will destroy Othello, and it is expressed in very graphic, psychological language: "I have't! It is engendered! Hell and night/ Must bring this monstrous birth to the world's light" (394–95). What exactly Iago's plan is we never learn, but even Iago seems to be impressed with the fact that this is a "monstrous birth" associated with hell. We are reminded of Hamlet's energetic stumbling upon the idea of the play within the play. It will not do to "fall a-cursing like a very drab,/ A scullion" (2.2.598–99). "Fie upon't, foh!" says Hamlet in disgust with himself, and then he immediately hits on a new idea: "About, my brains./ Hum—" (599–600). ("Hum" occurs only in Quarto 2.) At the end of fifteen lines of detailed speculation, Hamlet arrives at his conclusion: "The play's the thing/ Wherein I'll catch the conscience of the King" (616–17). This is much more fully worked out than anything Iago plans. Hamlet is obviously not a villain, but Shakespeare wants to show the spontaneous workings of both Hamlet's and Iago's minds.

From this point on, Iago plots by fits and starts. He picks up hints from the dramatic situation. Long before Cassio is dismissed from his lieutenancy because of a drunkenness engineered by Iago, which leads Cassio to ask Desdemona to intercede with Othello for him, Iago is already jumping at the chance of ensnaring Cassio in an imagined sexual relation with Desdemona. In Act II, scene i when Cassio innocently takes Desdemona's hand, Iago is instantly alert to the damaging possibilities. He says aside:

He takes her by the palm. Ay, well said, whisper! With as little a web as this will I ensnare as great a fly as Cassio. Ay, smile upon her, do! I will gyve thee in thine own courtship. (165–68)

It is interesting that in this passage Iago imagines himself as a spider catching Cassio in his web. This is only one among the many animal images that Iago (and all of Shakespeare's villains) use. "Gyve" (Folio "give") is a strong word meaning fetter or shackle, and although it makes for a mixed metaphor (with the spider's web), it works well for Iago's impetuous and strongly emotional aside.

Iago focuses on Cassio well before he begins to work on Othello. The soliloquy at the end of Act II, scene i gives us another fascinating insight into the way Iago's mind works. What is striking is how random Iago's thinking is. He seems to tell himself things that can't possibly be true (since we know that he has made them up beforehand). For example, the soliloquy begins: "That Cassio loves her, I do well believe 't" (286). Iago has no conceivable basis for saying this—it is something he himself has invented. The next line is even more problematical: "That she [Desdemona] loves him, 'tis apt and of great credit" (287). Why is it likely ("apt") and generally believed ("of great credit")? Of course, it isn't any of these things, and the intelligent Iago seems to be kidding himself.

Suddenly, we have what could be an amazing revelation (but it isn't):

Now I do love her too;
Not out of absolute lust, though peradventure
I stand accountant for as great a sin,
But partly led to diet my revenge,
For that I do suspect the lusty Moor
Hath leapt into my seat; the thought whereof
Doth, like a poisonous mineral, gnaw my inwards;
And nothing can or shall content my soul
Till I am evened with him, wife for wife. (291–99)

There are two wild assertions in this passage: (1) that Iago loves Desdemona, and (2) that Othello is cuckolding Iago with Emilia. We never hear anything further about either of these suppositions in the course of the play, and Iago goes to great lengths to convince Roderigo that Othello is not lusty at all. I think this soliloquy provides an excellent example of how Iago's mind works: his thinking is loose and associative, and he makes many random assertions that are never followed up. They are energetic and emotional, but also empty.

The soliloquy continues its focus on Cassio, as if he were Iago's real antagonist:

I'll have our Michael Cassio on the hip,
Abuse him to the Moor in the right garb
(For I fear Cassio with my nightcap too). . . . (305–7)

That Cassio is cuckolding him too is another wild assertion without any basis in the play.

Iago not only wants to undo Othello, but he wants Othello to be grateful to him:

Make the Moor thank me, love me, and reward me
For making him egregiously an ass
And practicing upon his peace and quiet,
Even to madness. (308–11)

Of course, this is what happens in the play, and Iago triumphs with a completeness that could not have been foreseen. Yet Iago in the course of the play just throws out hints and possibilities. He admits to himself: "'Tis here"—in other words that the elements of his plot are all in his mind—"but yet confused" (311). I think "confused" in this context is a strong word that means jumbled up, incoherent, scattered. Even Iago can't convince himself that he has a rational plan of attack.

In Act II, scene iii Iago makes Cassio drunk, and Othello dismisses Cassio from his lieutenancy. Iago's soliloquy toward the end of the scene follows the pattern of his other soliloquies, and it is noteworthy how important soliloquy is to him, certainly as important as it is to Hamlet. It also answers the question whether the soliloquizer always speaks the truth. Obviously he does not, since the soliloquies are spoken directly to the audience, who have no way of judging. The soliloquies do represent the character thinking out loud, but in Iago's case his thinking is full of misrepresentations and momentary lapses in speaking the truth. Iago, especially in the soliloquies, is often self-deluded.

In the soliloquy in Act II, scene iii, for example, we find him speaking again of Desdemona's "appetite" (347) as if she were a whore: "she's framed as fruitful/ As the free elements" (341–42). He will counsel Cassio that she asks for his reinstatement only to satisfy " her body's lust" (357). But the soliloquy ends with Iago once more asserting her essential goodness:

So will I turn her virtue into pitch,
And out of her own goodness, make the net
That shall enmesh them all. (360–62)

This is like Iago's soliloquy in Act IV, scene i: "And many worthy and chaste dames even thus,/ All guiltless, meet reproach" (48–49). Iago is in no doubt about what he is doing with Desdemona, but the plot against Othello takes shape with seeming inevitability.

In Iago's short soliloquy at the end of Act II, scene iii, there are further specific details about how he will proceed:

Two things are to be done:
My wife must move for Cassio to her mistress;
I'll set her on. . . . (382–84)

Thus Emilia is drawn into the plot. The next move is also clear:

> Myself awhile to draw the Moor apart
> And bring him jump when he may Cassio find
> Soliciting his wife. (385–87)

So Iago's plan is in progress. He congratulates himself on his own cleverness: "Ay, that's the way!/ Dull not device by coldness and delay" (387–88). We are already almost in the middle of the play, so Iago is aware, like Hamlet, of his own "coldness and delay." Things will now move more speedily, and we can no longer accuse Iago of dithering.

Desdemona's handkerchief (also called her "napkin") doesn't enter into the action until about the middle of the play in Act III, scene iii. Othello complains that he has a "pain upon my forehead" (283), meaning that he feels the horns popularly associated with being a cuckold. Desdemona offers to bind her husband's forehead with her napkin, but Othello complains that her "napkin is too little" (286). At this point Desdemona drops her handkerchief (the stage direction is supplied by Rowe), and Emilia picks it up when Othello and Desdemona exit a few lines later. The point of the handkerchief is that it is very important to Iago, as Emilia informs us: "My wayward husband hath a hundred times/ Wooed me to steal it" (291–92). We never learn why it is so significant for Iago, and we have to assume that it is one (among many) in the inventory of items in his rolling fantasy. He has no way of foreseeing at this point how effective the handkerchief is going to be. Emilia knows nothing of her husband's plans: "What he will do with it,/ Heaven knows, not I; nothing but to please his fantasy" (296–97). Here again we are made aware of Iago's "fantasy" (fancy or imagination), which Emilia interprets innocently as his whim or caprice, but we are aware of darker meanings.

He seizes on the handkerchief in a very sexualized discourse. Emilia keeps reminding us of how important it is to her husband: it is a thing "which so often you did bid me steal" (307). She wants to know "What will you do with't, that you have been so earnest/ To have me filch it" (312–13)? But Iago's reply is brusque: "Why, what is that to you?" (313). This implies that he doesn't yet know how he will use it. He says only: "I have use for it" (317), but in the soliloquy that follows Emilia's exit, he already has a plan: "I will in Cassio's lodging lose this napkin/ And let him [Cassio] find it" (318–19). Then Iago switches abruptly to Othello:

> Trifles light as air
> Are to the jealous confirmations strong
> As proofs of Holy Writ. This may do something.
> The Moor already changes with my poison. . . . (319–22)

Notice how tentative Iago is: "This *may* do something." He has no idea at this point how effective the handkerchief will be.

Iago doesn't even mention the handkerchief until more than a hundred lines later. When Othello says "I'll tear her all to pieces!" (428), Iago craftily urges patience:

Nay, yet be wise. Yet we see nothing done;
She may be honest yet. Tell me but this:
Have you not sometimes seen a handkerchief
Spotted with strawberries in your wife's hand? (429–32)

The details are sure to infuriate Othello, who replies: "I gave her such a one; 'twas my first gift" (433).

Iago does not proceed rashly, but he knows how to invent provocative details:

I know not that; but such a handkerchief—
I am sure it was your wife's—did I today
See Cassio wipe his beard with. (434–36)

How cleverly Iago now uses Cassio—more clever than Cassio's being only Desdemona's lover—to debase Othello's magical handkerchief for a very mundane use. Othello is beside himself: "If it be that—" (436). Iago skillfully stokes his rage: "If it be that, or any that was hers,/ It speaks against her with the other proofs" (437–38). How mock-cautious Iago is—the handkerchief is only one among many "other proofs." He is testing the waters here, but Othello's wild reaction displaces the need for any other proofs. The handkerchief now becomes Iago's major plot device.

From this point on, the handkerchief is a leitmotif in the play; it is mentioned at least two dozen times. In the next scene (III, iv) Desdemona is disturbed that she has lost it—she would rather have lost her "purse/Full of crusadoes" (25–26)—but she has no idea how momentous the loss is for her husband. Othello fetishizes the handkerchief; he endows it with magical properties. An Egyptian "charmer" (57), or magician, presented it to Othello's mother. It comes, however, with a curse, as the charmer explains:

while she kept it
'Twould make her amiable and subdue my father
Entirely to her love; but if she lost it
Or made a gift of it, my father's eye
Should hold her loathèd, and his spirits should hunt
After new fancies. (58–63)

It is Othello himself who elaborates on the mystic significance of the handkerchief so that Iago need say nothing further.

Othello needs to explicate in detail the symbolism; his mother

dying, gave it me,
And bid me, when my fate would have me wived,
To give it her [his wife]. I did so; and take heed on't. . . . (63–65)

The handkerchief is mythologized:

There's magic in the web of it.
A sibyl that had numbered in the world
The sun to course two hundred compasses,
In her prophetic fury sewed the work;
The worms were hallowed that did breed the silk,
And it was dyed in mummy which the skillful
Conserved of maidens' hearts. (69–75)

Desdemona is astounded by this passionate declaration of her husband. It is
at this point that she begins to feel the imminence of a tragic outcome. There
is no possibility of reasoning with Othello, who is so strongly manipulated
by Iago that he seems a villain. Through the workings of dramatic irony, the
audience (unlike Othello) knows what is really happening in the play, but
they can only compassionate with him as Iago relentlessly persuades him to
become a murderer.

References to the handkerchief still reverberate in the last scene of the
play (V, ii). There are six significant mentions. When Othello comes to murder his wife, Desdemona still can ask innocently: "What's the matter?" (47).
But Othello is preoccupied with "ocular proof" (3.3.357): "That handkerchief which I so loved and gave thee,/ Thou gav'st to Cassio" (5.2.48–49).
Desdemona has no opportunity to expostulate with her husband: "Send for
the man and ask him" (50). Every avenue of rational explanation is blocked.
Othello is so carried away with Iago's persuasions that he resorts to falsi-
fying: "By heaven, I saw my handkerchief in's hand!" (62), and again: "I
saw the handkerchief" (66). He is totally deluded by Iago and the extent of
his delusion is ferocious. When Desdemona suggests that Cassio may have
found it: "I never gave it him. Send for him hither./ Let him confess a truth"
(67–68). But Othello cannot be moved, and he even resorts to blatant lies to
strengthen his case:

Othello. He hath confessed.
Desdemona. What, my lord?
Othello. That he hath used thee. (68–70)

All these fearful speeches end when Othello smothers his wife (83 s.d.).

Even after he has murdered her and Emilia upbraids him for having "killed the sweetest innocent/ That e'er did lift up eye" (196–97), Othello still persists in retelling—with additional details—Iago's narrative about the handkerchief. Desdemona

> did gratify his [Cassio's] amorous works
> With that recognizance and pledge of love,
> Which first I gave her. I saw it in his hand.
> It was a handkerchief, an antique token
> My father gave my mother. (210–14)

The handkerchief is still the mythologized, maternal symbol of love.

Only Emilia can shake Othello's foolish confidence: "O thou dull Moor, that handkerchief thou speak'st of/ I found by fortune, and did give my husband" (222–23). But even this direct revelation does not sway Othello. He still needs to ask: "How came you, Cassio, by that handkerchief/ That was my wife's?" (315–16). It is only when Cassio says "I found it in my chamber" (316) that Othello acknowledges his folly: "O fool! Fool! Fool!" (319). This is the mystery, as Othello himself confesses, "Of one that loved not wisely, but too well" (340).

Finally, I would like to consider Iago's various styles as this relates to the way his villainy is so successfully accomplished. He is an excellent speaker, and he commands a wide variety of styles, so that he can be all things to all men while he wears his heart upon his sleeve and never reveals his purposes. In Act II, scene i while awaiting Othello's arrival in Cyprus, he entertains Desdemona with a witty, courtly, anti-feminine discourse, including a long string of couplets (seven pair) about different kinds of women:

> If she be fair and wise: fairness and wit,
> The one's for use, the other useth it. . . .
> If she be black, and thereto have a wit,
> She'll find a white that shall her blackness fit. (127–28, 130–31)

In Act II, scene iii the eloquent and facile Iago even sings two popular drinking songs.

But this is not his usual style. When he is trying to persuade Othello that he is a cuckold, Iago is wheedling, insinuating, questioning, fragmentary, hesitant, and repetitious as in Act III, scene iii. Iago is skillful in planting questions that stick in Othello's mind; for example: "Did Michael Cassio, when you wooed my lady,/ Know of your love?" (94–95). When Othello answers that he "went between us very oft" (100), Iago begins his circuitous planting of a doubt in Othello's mind:

Iago. Indeed?
Othello. Indeed? Ay, indeed! Discern'st thou aught in that?
Is he not honest?
Iago. Honest, my lord?
Othello. Honest? Ay, honest.
Iago. My lord, for aught I know. (101–4)

Iago is a specialist in saying nothing, in leaving crucial points suspended, so that Othello seems to be answering himself.

We see Othello slowly becoming more and more enraged, as he supplies the literal truth of what Iago cunningly conceals:

Othello. What dost thou think?
Iago. Think, my lord?
Othello. Think, my lord?
By heaven, thou echoest me,
As if there were some monster in thy thought
Too hideous to be shown. Thou dost mean something.
I heard thee say even now, thou lik'st not that,
When Cassio left my wife. What didst not like? (105–10)

Of course, Othello is no match, rhetorically, for the super-subtle Iago, who wears his heart upon his sleeve "For daws to peck at; I am not what I am" (1.1.62).

Like many of Shakespeare's villains, Iago can also be a plain speaker who prides himself on his close relation with the audience, as witnessed by his many soliloquies. In the first scene of the play we see Iago calling up to Brabantio his vile sexual accusations of Othello: "Even now, now, very now, an old black ram/ Is tupping your white ewe" (85–86). Iago is exaggeratedly dramatic and provocative with Desdemona's father as he is later with Othello: "Even now, now, very now." "Tupping" is a vulgar, animalistic word (like the vulgar Yiddish word "shtupping," which has entered New York discourse). It occurs only this once in Shakespeare.

A little further on, Iago elaborates his animal imagery:

you'll have your daughter covered with a Barbary horse, you'll have your nephews [grandsons] neigh to you, you'll have coursers for cousins, and gennets [small Spanish horses] for germans [blood relations]. (108–11)

"Covered" means copulated, specifically by a stallion, and "Barbary" refers to the coast of North Africa, where Moors are supposed to come from. Later in the play Desdemona sings "a song of 'Willow'" (4.3.28) learned from her mother's maid "called Barbary" (26). Iago concludes his sexual imagery in his next speech: "I am one, sir, that comes to tell you your daughter and the Moor are making the beast with two backs" (l.l.113–14). It is no wonder that Brabantio thinks, like Egeus in *A Midsummer Night's Dream*, that Othello must have used drugs to seduce his innocent Venetian daughter.

Iago's vocabulary is highly eroticized, mostly directed at Desdemona, and we remember that he is trying to convince not only Othello of Desdemona's whorishness but also Roderigo and Cassio. In Act II, scene i he is attempting to persuade Roderigo that the hot and young Desdemona will not continue long with the aging Othello, but will turn her appetite to the "salt and most hidden loose affection" (239–40) of Cassio. "When the blood is made dull with the act of sport, there should be game to inflame it and to give satiety a fresh appetite" (225–27). Iago makes very specific sexual promises to Roderigo. "Blood" in Renaissance physiology was thought to carry the sexual impulses, and the word is often repeated in *Othello*, as in Iago's "lust of the blood and a permission of the will" (1.3.330–1) and Othello's "Thy bed, lust-stained, shall with lust's blood be spotted" (5.1.36). "Blood" is one of Empson's complex words that combines the notions of sex and murder.[8] Iago's "act of sport" is echoed in many other places, for example in his sexual provocations of Cassio about Othello's wedding night: "He hath not yet made wanton the night with her, and she is sport for Jove" (2.3.16–17). Also it is found in Emilia's practical declarations to Desdemona about the sexual rights of women: "And have not we affections?/ Desires for sport? And frailty? As men have?" (4.3.103–4).

Like most of Shakespeare's villains, Iago puts great emphasis on his will. The word "will" has strong erotic associations, as we may see in Shakespeare's punning Sonnet 135: "Whoever hath her wish, thou hast thy *Will*,/ And *Will* to boot, and *Will* in overplus" (also in Sonnet 136). Iago upbraids Roderigo for speaking of his virtue:

> Virtue? A fig! 'Tis in ourselves that we are thus, or thus. Our bodies are our gardens, to the which our wills are gardeners; so that if we will plant nettles or sow lettuce, set hyssop and weed up thyme . . . why, the power and corrigible authority of this lies in our wills. (1.3.314–21)

This emphasis on the power of will is echoed by Edmund in *King Lear* and by the Bastard in *King John*. Through strength of will, powerful men can do whatever they want, an idea that has particular force in sexual matters.

Finally, I would like to look at what I consider a special locution of Iago: the word "ha." This is generally understood to be a meaningless expletive like the words "O," "pah," "foh," etc. "Ha, ha, ha" is used to indicate laughter in Shakespeare, but "ha" alone (or doubled) is an expression of surprise or astonishment. The most memorable example occurs as soon as Iago sees Cassio part with Desdemona: "Ha! I like not that" (3.3.35) This is a calculated provocation on Iago's part, since he equivocates when Othello presses him for an explanation:

> Cassio, my lord? No, sure, I cannot think it
> That he would steal away so guilty-like,
> Seeing your coming. (38–40)

Does Cassio indeed "steal away so guilty-like," or is Iago making everything up to poison Othello's mind? In *The Winter's Tale*, which is modeled on *Othello*, we could ask the same questions about what the jealous Leontes sees in relation to Hermione and Polixenes. Does he, for example, actually observe them "Kissing with inside lip" or "Horsing foot on foot" (1.2.285—288)? Like most of Shakespeare's villains, Iago is a consummate actor, and his meaningless expletive "ha" is full of accusatory overtones. "Ha" is a brilliant marker of the chaos Iago is sowing in Othello's mind, a chaos promoted by incessant questions, insinuations, hints, fragments, and non-answers.

The word "ha" echoes in Act III, scene iii (four uses), but the most significant occurrence is when Othello says "Ha!" at line 165. He is picking up Iago's word, and its use here marks how successful Iago is in convincing Othello of Desdemona's adultery. The context is crucial. Othello's previous speech expresses irritation that Iago does not answer his questions: "By heaven, I'll know thy thoughts!" (162), but Iago refuses any reply: "You cannot, if my heart were in your hand;/ Nor shall not whilst 'tis in my custody" (163–64). At the end of the play, Othello is still vainly pressing Iago for explanations, as he says to Cassio: "Will you, I pray, demand that demi-devil/ Why he hath thus ensnared my soul and body?" (5.2.297–98). But Iago still refuses to answer: "Demand me nothing. What you know, you know,/ From this time forth I never will speak word" (299–300). Of course, Iago has revealed very little about his motives in the course of the play, nor has he ever spelled out any of his insinuations. In this same scene Othello is still echoing Iago's word "ha," for example, in speaking of the strangled Desdemona: "Ha! No more moving?/ Still as the grave" (92–93) and in reaction to Emilia's accusation: "She was too fond of her most filthy bargain" (154), to which Othello can only exclaim in inexpressible grief: "Hah?" (155). He cannot believe the intense personal tragedy that has overtaken him.

Iago is a fluent and clever speaker and also a brilliant actor. There is only one place in the play where he is at a loss for words. When Othello is fully resolved to take Desdemona's life, he has a momentary pause in which at one and the same time he strengthens his determination and expresses his intense love. It feels proleptic, as if he already foresees his tragic error but can do nothing to stop the inevitable momentum. It is in this context that Iago doesn't seem to know what to do or say. When Othello exclaims: "A fine woman, a fair woman, a sweet woman?" (4.1.180–81), Iago can only reply: "Nay, you must forget that" (182). He seems to have lost the initiative. Again, when Othello declares: "O, the world hath not a sweeter creature! She might lie by an emperor's side and command him tasks" (185–87), Iago's riposte is feeble: "Nay, that's not your way" (188), or when he speaks again: "She's the worse for all this" (193). To Othello's intense cry for compassion: "But yet the pity of it, Iago. O Iago, the pity of it, Iago" (197–98), Iago has no suitable answer: "If you are so fond over her iniquity, give her patent to offend; for if it touch not you, it comes near nobody" (199–201). This answer sounds merely petulant and cranky, since Iago of course is entirely lacking in compassion, nor does he have any way of understanding Othello's "pity of it." Othello once more, momentarily, reasserts his eloquence and goodness of heart.

We began with Iago as Shakespeare's archetypal villain because he is so diabolically clever and such a wonderful actor. As he tells the poor dupe Roderigo, "Thou know'st we work by wit, and not by witchcraft" (2.3.372). This is a key statement of Iago's practice. "Wit" had a much wider range of meanings in Shakespeare's time than in ours. Its basic meaning is probably intelligence. Iago is quick, and he is much more an improviser than a determined and careful plotter. He picks up bits and pieces of information and suddenly sees where they can be useful. He knows that the handkerchief should be counted among "Trifles light as air" (3.3.319), but he sees to his own surprise how important it is to Othello. The handkerchief doesn't enter into his plotting until well into the play, and it has a fortuitous quality, since Emilia accidentally finds it. The truth of the matter is that Iago doesn't need the handkerchief. He could easily have driven Othello to a kind of murderous madness with something else. Like the Vice figure, Iago has an element of sport or game in all of his proceedings, as there is in many of the villains we will discuss. Iago wants to make sure the audience knows that Roderigo is not his friend or boon companion. He is his "fool," a "snipe" (a proverbially foolish and easily caught bird), from whom he takes money and jewels to further his supposed suit to Desdemona, all of which is done for Iago's "sport and profit" (1.3.377). These words are spoken in Iago's first soliloquy, very early in the play and well before his action against Othello even begins. This is chilling but also predictive.

NOTES

1. See Robert B. Heilman, *Magic in the Web: Action and Language in Othello*, Lexington, KY: University of Kentucky Press, 1956, for a detailed, sensitive close reading of Iago's role, based chiefly on imagery. See also Stanley Edgar Hyman,

"Untuning the Othello Music: Iago as Stage Villain," in *The Rarer Action: Essays in Honor of Francis Fergusson*, ed. Alan Cheuse and Richard Koffler, New Brunswick, NJ: Rutgers University Press, 1970, pp. 55–67, for a connection between Iago and the English morality plays (similar to the thesis of Bernard Spevack, *Shakespeare and the Allegory of Evil*, New York, NY: Columbia University Press, 1958). which is also the theme of the excellent short book of Maik Goth, *From Chaucer's Pardoner to Shakespeare's Iago*, Frankfurt: Peter Langs 2009. See also S. L. Bethell, "Shakespeare's Imagery: The Diabolic Images in *Othello*," *Shakespeare Survey*, 5 (1952), 62–80. Marvin Rosenberg has an original, performative approach to Iago in "In Defense of Iago," *Shakespeare Quarterly*, 6 (1955), 45–58; see also his *The Masks of Othello*, Berkeley, CA: University of California Press, 1961.

2. See Samuel Taylor Coleridge, *Shakespearean Criticism*, ed. Thomas Middleton Raysor, 2 vols., London, 1960, I, 44. There is a searching article by Sylvan Barnet: "Coleridge on Shakepeare's Villains," *Shakespeare Quarterly*, 7 (1956), 9–20. See also Robert Langbaum's wide-ranging article, "Character Versus Action in Shakespeare," *Shakespeare Quarterly*, 8 (1957), 57–69, on nineteenth century, Romantic readings of Shakespeare.

3. See Caroline F. E. Spurgeon, *Shakespeare's Imagery and What it Tells Us*, New York, 1935. See also Edward A. Armstrong, *Shakespeare's Imagination*, rev. ed., Lincoln, NE: University of Nebraska Press, 1963. Armstrong discusses the dogs-licking-candy image cluster.

4. See Charlotte Spivack, *The Comedy of Evil on Shakespeare's Stage*, Madison, N.J.: Fairleigh Dickinson University Press, 1978, especially Ch. 6. See also Molly Smith, *The Darker World Within: Evil in the Tragedies of Shakespeare and His Successors*, Newark, DE: University of Delaware Press, 1991, for a New Historical interpretation indebted to Greenblatt. See also Tom McAlindon, "The Evil of Play and the Play of Evil: Richard, Iago and Edmund Contextualized," in *Shakespeare's Universe: Essays in Honour of W. R. Elton*, London, Scolar Press, 1996, pp. 148–54. McAlindon sees Shakespeare as indebted to ideas about the devil rather than the Vice. See also Maik Goth, *From Chaucer's Pardoner to Shakespeare's Iago*, which attempts to deal with Iago's love of "sport."

5. See William Empson's subtle discussion, "Honest in *Othello*," in *The Structure of Complex Words*, London, 1951, Chapter 11.

6. In his Arden edition (London, 1997), E. A. J. Honigmann comments very well on this point: "Iago also speaks for Shakespeare. Attempting to manipulate the other characters, Iago is the dramatist inside the play; in soliloquy he weighs the options for his plot, as Shakespeare must have done, and no doubt his delight in his creative brilliance was shared by his only begetter" (p. 105).

7. Edward Pechter has very original things to say about Iago in Chapter 3 of *Othello and Interpretive Traditions*, Iowa City, IA: University of Iowa Press, 1999; for example, he notes: "The more we see of Iago the less sense he makes. Despite his self-congratulatory rationality, he is full of contradictions" (p. 62).

8. See William Empson, *The Structure of Complex Words*, London, 1951.

Chapter 2

Tarquin and Aaron

We began with Iago as Shakespeare's archetypal villain, who sums up the qualities of many previous villains. I would like to proceed now with a discussion that is more or less chronological, beginning with Tarquin in *The Rape of Lucrece* and Aaron in *Titus Andronicus*. I think we find that Shakespeare, very early in his career, started to think of the villain in specific ways, probably related to the Vice figure in the morality plays that Bernard Spevack discusses so rewardingly in *Shakespeare and the Allegory of Evil* (New York, 1958). To turn the discussion the other way around, Tarquin and Aaron are both villains whose traits are more fully developed in Iago.

The Rape of Lucrece and *Titus Andronicus* were probably written very close to each other in the early 1590's; it cannot convincingly be determined which came first.[1] Tarquin is surprisingly well developed as a dramatic character. Although he is certain that the rape of Lucrece is wrong, he is powerfully motivated to exercise his will. His debate with himself has all the rudiments of dramatic conflict. Without any mitigation, he knows that what he plans to do is loathsome, so that when he considers the moral issues it seems as if he is trying to convince himself not to do a deed that will stain his honor forever:

> And die, unhallowed thoughts, before you blot
> With your uncleanness that which is divine.
> Offer pure incense to so pure a shrine.
> Let fair humanity abhor the deed
> That spots and stains love's modest snow-white weed. (192–96)

He is sure of his own debasement: "A martial man to be soft fancy's slave" (200).

His anticipation of a momentary sexual pleasure is similar to the intense disillusionment of Sonnet 129, "Th'expense of spirit in a waste of shame." Tarquin is interesting as a tragic figure because he is so clear-sighted about the limitations of the sexual fulfillment he so avidly seeks:

> What win I if I gain the thing I seek?
> A dream, a breath, a froth of fleeting joy.
> Who buys a minute's mirth to wail a week?
> Or sells eternity to get a toy [trifle]? (211–14)

He has none of Troilus's transcendental yearnings in *Troilus and Cressida* after a joy that is teasingly transient. Tarquin engages in a moral debate, a "disputation/'Tween frozen conscience and hot-burning will" (246–47). We know how it will end, but we are engaged by his conscience, which hardly seems frozen at this point. It is actively in play.

The debate soon comes to an end as Tarquin asserts his manly, military, youthful will: "Affection is my captain" (271) and not reason: "Desire my pilot is, beauty my prize;/Then who fears sinking where such treasure lies?" (279–80). There is a strong emphasis on will (as opposed to reason), as there is in Shakespeare's sonnets 135 and 136 (with extensive puns on Shakespeare's name, Will). Tarquin speaks of his will as if it were an inevitable force that Lucrece cannot possibly resist: "thou with patience must my will abide,/ My will that marks thee for my earth's delight" (486–87). In this dualistic argument, he speaks of his will as something over which even he himself has no control: "But Will is deaf, and hears no heedful friends;/Only he hath an eye to gaze on Beauty" (495–96). He allegorizes and personifies his Will (a rhetorical strategy that Lucrece is overly fond of later in the poem). Tarquin addresses apostrophes to himself. There is a strong emphasis on military imagery, as if he were the conqueror laying siege to Lucrece's beauty. He is "come to scale/ Thy never-conquered fort" (481–82).

Tarquin also uses a good deal of animal imagery to define his aggressive, manly purpose, and this creates a model for many of Shakespeare's villains. His sword is "like a falcon tow'ring in the skies" (506). He is like the cockatrice or basilisk, the fabulous creature with a "dead-killing eye" (540). (Compare Aaron's "deadly-standing eye" in *Titus Andronicus* 2.3.32, another basilisk allusion.) Lucrece like a "weak mouse panteth" (555), while Tarquin, the "foul night-walking cat" (554), dallies with her. Her serious behavior only "feeds his vulture folly" (556). Later on Tarquin is a "wolf" (677), a "full-fed hound or gorgèd hawk" (694), a "thievish dog"(736), a "wand'ring wasp" (839), a canker "worm" (848), a cuckoo, and a toad (849–50)—all animals and insects connected with destructive and disgusting prey. Tarquin is not literally a murderer in this narrative, but he in effect kills Lucrece when he chooses to rape her. This is another continuing theme for villains: they tend to be either killers or without any scruples about killing to accomplish their purposes.

In the Troy tapestry that Lucrece describes in such detail, the duplicitous Sinon in the Trojan horse is compared with Tarquin:

> For even as subtile Sinon here is painted,
> So sober-sad, so weary, and so mild
> (As if with grief or travail he had fainted),
> To me came Tarquin armèd, to beguiled [beguile]
> With outward honesty, but yet defiled
> With inward vice. As Priam him did cherish,
> So did I Tarquin; so my Troy did perish. (1541–47)

Like Tarquin, Sinon is a "confirmèd devil" (1513) who hides his "secret evil" (1515). He is "perjured Sinon, whose enchanting story/The credulous old Priam after slew" (1521–22). It is the false appearance of Sinon that deeply disturbs Lucrece: "So fair a form lodged not a mind so ill" (1530). She somehow holds herself at fault, like Priam, for not being able to see through Tarquin (here analogized with Sinon). But Priam, like Lucrece, was won over by Sinon's seemingly truthful narrative.

It is only a short step from Tarquin and Sinon in *The Rape of Lucrece* to Aaron in *Titus Andronicus*.[2] Titus remembers Tarquin when Lavinia uses a copy of Ovid's *Metamorphoses* to compare her own rape and dismemberment with that of Philomena, which is of course the source story for the rape of Lucrece. Titus thinks mistakenly that it was Saturnine "as Tarquin erst,/ That left the camp to sin in Lucrece' bed" (4.1.63–64). Later in the scene Marcus refers to Brutus, who swore to take revenge for the rape of "that chaste dishonored dame" (90). These references suggest that Shakespeare was thinking of *The Rape of Lucrece* while he was writing *Titus Andronicus* (or vice versa)—the rapes of Lucrece and Lavinia are conceptually quite close.

What allies Aaron with Iago is his jocularity, a term that Spevack uses to trace the origin of Shakespeare's villains in the Vice figure of the morality plays. Very early in *Othello*, Iago tells Roderigo that if he can cuckold Othello "thou dost thyself a pleasure, me a sport" (1.3.364–65), and a few lines further in his soliloquy Iago assures the audience that he is only spending time with such a "snipe" as Roderigo "for my sport and profit" (377). The word "sport" is eroticized when Iago speaks of intercourse as "the act of sport" (2.1.226) and Desdemona herself as "sport for Jove" (2.3.17).

Similarly, in his proud recital of his deeds in Act V, scene i, Aaron uses "sport" as a sexual word for the rape and dismemberment of Lavinia:

> Why, she was washed, and cut, and trimmed, and 'twas
> Trim sport for them which had the doing of it. (95–96)

Aaron puns mercilessly on "trim," which is both a barber's term and a familiar adjective meaning fine, nice, or pretty. He is thoroughly enjoying himself in his shockingly original and expansive discourse, which Lucius questions: "O detestable villain! Call'st thou that trimming?" (94) Aaron is proud of his verbal dexterity. When Titus cuts off his own right hand in a futile effort to redeem his sons from death, Aaron also thinks of this event as "sport":

> And when I told the Empress of this sport,
> She sounded [swooned] almost at my pleasing tale,
> And for my tidings gave me twenty kisses. (118–20)

Beyond the idea of evil deeds as sport—and "sport" is also a favorite word of Puck in Act III, scene ii of *A Midsummer Night's Dream*—Aaron overreaches Iago in his own hearty laughter at his clever exploits. By way of confession, he tells Lucius:

> I played the cheater for thy father's hand,
> And when I had it drew myself apart,
> And almost broke my heart with extreme laughter.
> I pried me through the crevice of a wall,
> When for his hand he had his two sons' heads;
> Beheld his tears and laughed so heartily
> That both mine eyes were rainy like to his. . . . (111–17)

A "cheater" is an escheater, an officer appointed to look after property forfeited to the King (with a pun on the usual sense of "cheat"). This is a high point for Aaron in the play. He is thoroughly enjoying his own gleeful account of his adventures and how shocking all of this is to his hearers. Aaron's speech sounds like the vaunting of Barrabas and Ithamore in Marlowe's *Jew of Malta*, a play written just a few years before *Titus* (around 1592). This is the essence of Shakespeare's black comedy.

If we go back to the scene itself (III,i), we see Aaron at his most sardonic, which is a good word for him because it includes ideas of bitterness, scorn, and mockery. Titus, distracted by grief, speaks to Aaron as a trusted friend (as Othello does to Iago):

> With all my heart, I'll send the Emperor my hand.
> Good Aaron, wilt thou help to chop it off? (160–61)

Aaron is delighted with the irony and says aside:

> If that be called deceit, I will be honest,
> And never whilst I live deceive men so:
> But I'll deceive you in another sort,
> And that you'll say, ere half an hour pass.
> *He cuts off Titus' hand.* (188–91)

There is again the adjective "honest," a favorite word for Iago and for Brutus, too, in Antony's funeral oration in *Julius Caesar*.

In another soliloquy before he exits, Aaron expresses pure pleasure at his ingenious scheme: "O, how this villainy/ Doth fat me with the very thought of it!" (203). "Fat" means to make fat or to nourish. Aaron is really enjoying himself, as he expresses it in this triumphant couple when he exits:

> Let fools do good, and fair men call for grace,
> Aaron will have his soul black like his face. (204–5)

Aaron is, of course, joking when he speaks of his soul because he makes it clear in the play that he is an atheist,[3] as are many villains in Shakespeare, most notably Edmund, whose goddess is Nature. Iago, too, is certainly a firm believer in Nature rather than in anything even vaguely religious.

The point is made explicitly in Act V, scene i. Aaron tells Lucius that he shall not reveal any of his deeds unless Lucius swears that his black baby shall live. Lucius asks the obvious question:

> Who should I swear by? Thou believest no god:
> That granted, how canst thou believe an oath? (71–72)

Aaron acknowledges that he is non-believer, but he teases Lucius about his conscience, which seems very Catholic in this exchange:

> What if I do not? As indeed I do not;
> Yet, for I know thou art religious,
> And hast a thing within thee callèd conscience,
> With twenty popish tricks and ceremonies,
> Which I have seen thee careful to observe,

> Therefore I urge thy oath; for that I know
> An idiot holds his bauble for a god,
> And keeps the oath which by that god he swears. . . . (73–80)

Nothing further is said about Lucius's religion, but he does swear "by my god" (86) that he will protect Aaron's black baby. Even though Aaron doesn't believe in any god, he likes the ceremony of swearing. He is a devotee of Nature.

At the very end of the play, Marcus speaks of Aaron as "that misbelieving Moor" (5.3.143), and Lucius pronounces a horrible judgment on him, but Aaron's last speech is boastingly defiant:

> I am no baby, I, that with base prayers
> I should repent the evils I have done:
> Ten thousand worse than ever yet I did
> Would I perform, if I might have my will:
> If one good deed in all my life I did,
> I do repent it from my very soul. (185–90)

Aaron is a self-promoting creature of will who rejects totally Christian prayer and repentance. His final speech sounds like a kind of heroic vaunting that Iago never indulges in.

Aaron, like Othello, is a Moor, but in this play an important distinction is made between the civilized Romans and the uncivilized Goths and Moors. The difference is enunciated in the first scene, when Marcus exhorts his brother Titus to allow for the burial of his son Mutius (whom Titus has slain) in the family tomb: "Thou art a Roman, be not barbarous" (379). In other words, Titus must adhere to a high moral standard, just as Cleopatra the Egyptian claims that she will commit suicide "after the high Roman fashion/ And make death proud to take us" (*Antony and Cleopatra* 4.15.86–87). Aaron is a Moor, a "barbarous Moor" (2.3.78 and 5.3.4), "coal-black" (4.2.99) like his infant son—also "coal-black" like the mad Titus's fly (3.2.78)—but there is no mention made of his being from Africa. He enters the play in the first scene as a prisoner of war in Titus's triumphal procession, along with Tamora, the Queen of the Goths, and her three sons.

We learn from his Marlovian soliloquy in Act II, scene i that Tamora is Aaron's mistress:

> whom thou in triumph long
> Hast prisoner held, fettered in amorous chains,
> And faster bound to Aaron's charming eyes
> Than is Prometheus tied to Caucasus. (14–17)

There is parade of classical allusions and quotations (or near quotations) in Shakespeare's first Roman play. After Aaron's black baby is born, he takes it to the Goths, "There to dispose this treasure in mine arms,/And secretly to greet the Empress' friends" (4.2.174–75). The child will be brought up close to nature, since Aaron himself is a natural man without any religious beliefs:

> I'll make you feed on berries and on roots,
> And feed on curds and whey, and suck the goat,
> And cabin in a cave. . . . (178–80)

This sounds like the misogynistic Timon in *Timon of Athens* after he has fled Athens to live in the woods. In Act V, scene i Aaron is captured by a soldier of the Goths, now led by Lucius, the exiled son of Titus.

As a "misbelieving" (5.3.143), "irreligious" (121) Moor, Aaron trusts only in his own will. Like many of Shakespeare's villains, Aaron speaks in a familiar, colloquial, style that often uses vulgar, sexual words. For example, when he is advising Chiron and Demetrius, the sons of Tamora, on how to rape and mutilate Lavinia, he proceeds immediately to the heart of their dilemma:

> Why then, it seems, some certain snatch or so
> Would serve your turns.
> *Chiron.* Ay, so the turn were served.
> *Demetrius.* Aaron, thou hast hit it.
> *Aaron.* Would you had hit it too,
> Then should not we be tired with this ado. (2.1.95–98)

Both Jonathan Bate, the Arden editor of the Third Series. and J. C. Maxwell, the previous Arden editor, note the bawdy context without noting that "snatch" is a current slang term for the vulva or vagina (*Random House Dictionary*, 2 ed., meaning 13). "Turn" and "hit" are also specifically sexual terms. The Messenger reporting Antony's marriage to Octavia answers Cleopatra's "For what good turn?" with "For the best turn i' th' bed" (*Antony and Cleopatra* 2.5.58–59). "Hit" is used very often in Shakespeare with sexual innuendo (to hit a target), nowhere more repeatedly than in the wit combat in *Love's Labor's Lost* (4.1.120–30).

Even Chiron and Demetrius seem shocked by Aaron's aggressive vulgarity in Act IV, scene ii when the birth of Aaron and Tamora's black baby is revealed. Demetrius asks the obvious question: "Villain, what hast thou done?," to which Aaron replies curtly: "That which thou canst not undo." But Chiron insists on spelling out the public shame: "Thou hast undone our mother." But the jokey Aaron has the last, punning word: "Villain, I have done thy mother" (73–76). *Antony and Cleopatra,* too, has many eroticized references to "doing it" ("do't" at 1.1.38, 1.2.79, and 4.15.86).

Like all of Shakespeare's villains, Aaron uses significant animal imagery, which links him to man's animal nature. Without any speeches or moral reflections, he kills the Nurse who announces the delivery of his black baby as if he were sticking a pig. Only the Empress, the Nurse, and the midwife know of its existence, so Aaron acts decisively to dispose of the witnesses:

> Go to the Empress, tell her this I said.
> *He kills her.*
> Wheak, wheak!
> So cries a pig preparèd to the spit. (4.2.145–47)

This is the jocular Aaron thoroughly enjoying himself by a sudden stabbing right on stage. "Wheak, wheak" imitates the squealing of a stuck pig. It's the only occurrence of this word in Shakespeare and a sign of Aaron's mimetic, linguistic energy.

In the final scene, Lucius calls Aaron "This ravenous tiger" (5.3.5) as he does Tamora (195), and Aaron is also an "inhuman dog" (14). Earlier, Demetrius called Aaron a "hellish dog" (4.2.77), but Aaron is proud of this connection. In boastfully revealing his dark deeds to Lucius, Aaron seeks praise for his tutoring of Chiron and Demetrius in their rape and dismemberment of Lavinia:

> That bloody mind, I think, they learned of me,
> As true a dog as ever fought at head. (5.1.100–1)

J. C. Maxwell quotes Dr. Johnson's explanation that this is a reference to bulldogs seizing the bull by the nose,[4] but it may also be a more familiar reference to the brave dogs in the bloody sport of bear-baiting. Aaron always thinks that his diabolical deeds are praiseworthy. When a Goth soldier asks: "What, canst thou say all this and never blush?," Aaron refers him to the familiar proverb: "Ay, like the black dog, as the saying is" (121–22). "To blush like a black dog" (Tilley D507) was proverbial for brazenness and impudence. We remember Roderigo's anguished cry when Iago stabs him: "O damned Iago! O inhuman dog!" (5.1.62). As Armstrong points out, dogs generally have negative connotations in Shakespeare.[5]

Aaron, like Iago and many of Shakespeare's villains, is a plotter who takes particular pleasure in his schemes and stratagems. They are a product of his vivid imagination, as the play itself is the product of Shakespeare's imagination. This link between villain and author is a puzzling but teasing element in all of Shakespeare's works. "Policy" (and "politic" and "politician") are key words for many of Shakespeare's villains. Aaron uses "policy" only twice, but both occurrences are significantly negative. In his advice to Chiron and Demetrius on how to rape and dismember Lavinia, "'Tis policy and stratagem must do/ That you affect" (2.1.104–5). In other words they must be cunning and crafty and not direct in their pursuit of Lavinia. "Policy" was the word associated with the popular Renaissance idea of Machiavellianism, derived loosely from the chilling doctrines of machiavelli's *The Prince* (written in 1513 and translated into English in 1640, but notorious popular for its diabolic doctrines). When Aaron kills the Nurse who announces the birth of his and Tamora's black baby, he calls it

a deed of policy!
Shall she live to betray this guilt of ours?
A long-tongued babbling gossip? No, lords, no. (4.2.149–51)

This murder is just the right thing for a politic villain to do.

The *Oxford English Dictionary* defines "policy" in its "bad sense" as political expediency: "cunning, craftiness, dissimulation" (sense 4). The word is especially associated with Polonius in *Hamlet*, who "hunts the trail of policy" (2.2.47). After Hamlet kills him, he declares satirically that "A certain convocation of politic worms are e'en at him" (4.3.19–21). In *Coriolanus*, the protagonist protests against his mother's equivocating desire to combine "Honor and policy" (3.2. 42; also 46–48). In *Timon of Athens*, the First Stranger comments like a chorus on the cynical indifference of Timon's so-called friends: "For policy sits above conscience" (3.2.92). In *The Taming of the Shrew*, Petruchio boasts that his plan for the taming of Kate seems to be working: "Thus have I politicly begun my reign" (4.1.182). I could go on with many further citations, but "policy," "politic," and related words are used frequently by Shakespeare with strongly negative connotations.

Like "policy," "practice" is another word associated with villains. Tamora dressed as Revenge is sure that she can trick Titus, who she believes is mad:

I'll find some cunning practice out of hand [at once],
To scatter and disperse the giddy Goths,
Or at the least make them his enemies. (5.2.77–79)

A "practice" is a scheme or stratagem, as in the case of Laertes, killed with his own "Unbated and envenomed" rapier (*Hamlet* 5.2.318): "The foul practice/ Hath turned itself on me" (318–19). In *King Lear* Edmund concocts a speech for his brother Edgar about his "plot and damned practice" (2.1.73) against his father. And in *Othello*, Iago's second speech in the play looks to the future in the words he uses to condemn Cassio: "Mere prattle without practice/ Is all his soldiership" (1.1.23–24). Iago's boasted "practice," or practical knowledge, leads to the deaths of Othello, Desdemona, Roderigo, and Emilia. There is an implicit pun on "practice" throughout the play.

The Rape of Lucrece is not a subtle poem, but Tarquin is remarkable for his struggles with his conscience. Of course, his will to rape Lucrece overpowers his conscience, but this occurs seemingly without Tarquin wishing it. There is no doubt that he is a villain—perhaps Shakespeare's first portrait of a villain—and he has many of the characteristics that we will see in later villains. Aaron is a particularly vigorous and energetic dramatic character, who is notable as a laughing villain, laughing and sardonic. Not only is he not penitent at the end of *Titus Andronicus*, but he remembers that when Titus let him cut his hand off supposedly to save his sons, he "almost broke my heart with extreme laughter" (5.1.113). He seems to be influenced by the villains in Marlowe, especially in *The Jew of Malta*. Aaron is noteworthy as a strikingly colloquial speaker. Again, there is a great deal in Aaron that we find later in Iago, who is also a Moor, as well as in Richard, Duke of Gloucester, and Edmund.

NOTES

1. See Introduction to the third Aden edition of *Titus Andronicus* ed. Jonathan Bate, London, Routledge, 1995.

2. See Maurice Charney, *Titus Andronicus*, Harvester New Critical Introductions to Shakespeare, New York, 1990, for a detailed account of Aaron's role in the play.

3. See the comprehensive article by Earl Dachslager, "'The Stock of Barabbas': Shakespeare's Unfaithful Villains," *Upstart Crow*, 6 (1986), 8–21. Dachslager views atheists in the wider context of infidels.

4. See J. C. Maxwell's Arden edition of *Titus Andronicus*, London, 1961, p. 106.

5. See Edward A. Armstrong, *Shakespeare's Imagination*, rev. ed., Lincoln, NE: University of Nebraska Press, 1963.

Chapter 3

Richard, Duke of Gloucester

Richard, Duke of Gloucester (later King Richard III), first appears in the fifth act of *2 Henry VI*, but is more fully developed in *3 Henry VI* and *Richard III*. If these plays were written in the early 1590's, Richard is Shakespeare's most successful protagonist to date. He has many resemblances to Marlowe's Tamburlaine of a few years earlier, especially in his energetic style. Richard may well have been conceived right before Aaron and Tarquin. In any case, Richard offers a model for the Shakespearean villain, and many of his characteristics can be seen in Iago and other later villains.[1]

Richard's physical deformity is insisted on in all three plays.[2] Already in Act V of *2 Henry VI*, before Richard is even named Duke of Gloucester, Clifford calls him a "foul indigested lump,/ As crooked in thy manners as thy shape!" (157–58). "Indigested" is a strong word for formlessness and shapelessness, as the new born bear cub is "indigest" until it is licked into shape by its mother. Sonnet 114 equates "monsters, and things indigest," and in *King John* Salisbury comforts Prince Henry, the son of the poisoned and soon-to-be mad king, who was created "To set a form upon that indigest/ Which he [King John] hath left so shapeless and so rude" (5.7.26–27). In *3 Henry VI*, just before Richard stabs him, King Henry curses him, who at his birth was

an indigested and deformèd lump,
Not like the fruit of such a goodly tree.
Teeth hadst thou in thy head when thou was born
To signify thou cam'st to bite the world. . . . (5.6.51–54)

That Richard was born with teeth is repeated many times. After he has stabbed King Henry, his soliloquy in this same passage indicates his unnatural birth:

I came into the world with my legs forward.
Had I not reason, think ye, to make haste
And seek their ruin that usurped our right?
The midwife wondered, and the women cried
"O Jesus bless us, he is born with teeth!"
And so I was, which plainly signified
That I should snarl and bite and play the dog. (71–77)

Richard is proud of his monstrous birth, which marks him as an unmitigated villain. He is superior to other men, as figured in his special birth.

There is a similar passage in what the young Duke of York (whom Richard will have murdered in the Tower) says about his uncle, who "grew so fast/ That he could gnaw a crust at two hours old" (*Richard III* 2.4.27–28). Queen Margaret warns Buckingham to take heed of Richard's "venom tooth," which "will rankle to the death" (1.3.290). Richard's teeth not only bite, but they are also poisonous.

To return to the passage in *2 Henry VI*, Young Clifford calls Richard "Foul stigmatic" (5.1.215), an unusual word referring to a criminal branded with a hot iron, but the *Oxford English Dictionary* also defines it as "Marked with or having a deformity or blemish; deformed, ill-favoured, ugly" (sense 3). This extended meaning is clearly what Queen Margaret has in mind when she calls Richard

a foul misshapen stigmatic,
Marked by the Destinies to be avoided,
As venom toads, or lizards' dreadful stings. (*3 Henry VI* 2.3.136–38)

Again we should note how strongly Richard's physical deformity is linked with biting and poisonous animals.

Perversely, Richard seems proud of his defective body, as if this sets him apart from other men. He speaks about his infirmities with a gleeful energy that borders on heroic vaunting. All of this is emphasized in his many long soliloquies, in which he confides in the audience and seems to depend on their friendship and manly sympathy. Richard's extended soliloquy at the end of Act III, scene ii of *3 Henry VI* prepares us for his brilliant opening soliloquy in *Richard III*. He goes into great detail about how Love

forswore me in my mother's womb:
And, for I should not deal in her soft laws,
She did corrupt frail Nature with some bribe,
To shrink mine arm up like a withered shrub;
To make an envious [spiteful] mountain on my back,

Where sits deformity to mock my body;
To shape my legs of an unequal size;
To disproportion me in every part,
Like to a chaos, or an unlicked bear-whelp
That carries no impression like the dam. (153–62)

Richard goes into great detail about his missshapen body Love is personified as if it were Richard's enemy.

It's significant how detailed Richard's diatribe against Love is. Like Marlowe's Doctor Faustus, Richard reviews the pleasures that the world affords:

I'll make my heaven in a lady's lap,
And deck my body in gay ornaments
And witch [bewitch] sweet ladies with my words and looks. (148–50)

But the conclusion to his list of physical deformities prevents that choice:

And am I then a man to be beloved?
O monstrous fault, to harbor such a thought! (163–64)

Of course, the reasoning is specious—and we are wrong to think that sentiments expressed in soliloquy are necessarily true, especially for Shakespeare's villains. All of Richard's elaborate reasoning is merely a rationalization for his ambition. He will not be satisfied

Until my misshaped trunk that bears this head
Be round impalèd with a glorious crown. (170–71)

Again, in Richard's long soliloquy after he has murdered King Henry VI, there is a close connection between his deformity and his rejection of love:

Then, since the heavens have shaped my body so,
Let hell make crook'd my mind to answer it.
I have no brother, I am like no brother;
And this word "love," which graybeards call divine,
Be resident in men like one another
And not in me: I am myself alone. (5.6.78–83)

Richard sounds like Iago here, another misogynistic villain incapable of love. In the first scene of *Othello* Iago is already declaring "I am not what I am" (62) and separating himself from everyone else in the play. Richard immediately turns his attention to the murder of his brother Clarence.

Richard's opening soliloquy in *Richard III* continues the same themes that were well developed in *3 Henry VI*, which would support the argument that the *Henry VI* plays and *Richard III* are a coherent tetralogy. At the least, there is a strong connection between *Richard III* and *3 Henry VI*. Richard sees "Grim-visaged War" as capering "nimbly in a lady's chamber/ To the lascivious pleasing of a lute" (9, 12–13), but his physical deformity determines that he is "not shaped for sportive tricks/ Nor made to court an amorous looking glass" (14–15). "Sportive" is used in its sexual sense, as is the word "tricks."

He then goes on to catalogue his own ugliness as if he were proud of his special status. It is self-pity, but highly ironic and sardonic:

> I, that am rudely stamped, and want love's majesty
> To strut before a wanton ambling nymph;
> I, that am curtailed of this fair proportion,
> Cheated of feature by dissembling Nature,
> Deformed, unfinished, sent before my time
> Into this breathing world scarce half made up,
> And that so lamely and unfashionable
> That dogs bark at me as I halt by them;
> Why, I, in this weak piping time of peace,
> Have no delight to pass away the time,
> Unless to spy my shadow in the sun
> And descant on mine own deformity. (16–27)

Which he is doing right now at some length! Richard's ideas about love are characteristically distorted, as Iago's are. There is no "wanton ambling nymph" in this play or in any of the *Henry VI* plays.

Right after this soliloquy, Richard complains to Clarence that he is sent to prison by the machinations of Lady Grey, the wife of King Edward IV, Richard's brother:

> Why, this it is when men are ruled by women.
> 'Tis not the King that sends you to the Tower.
> My Lady Grey his wife, Clarence, 'tis she
> That tempers him to this extremity. (62–65)

Of course, this is a lie. Richard is the one who sends his brother to the Tower and has him killed by paid assassins. Like many of Shakespeare's villains, especially Iago and Edmund, Richard is a misogynist. That is part of his determination to act alone without any ties to others, especially to women.

Let us return to Richard's opening soliloquy. According to his specious reasoning:

And therefore, since I cannot prove a lover
To entertain these fair well-spoken days,
I am determinèd to prove a villain
And hate the idle pleasures of these days. (28–31)

Here is Richard again as the enemy of pleasure. His soliloquy confides to the audience that he is a villain, and he goes into detail about his ingenious plot to kill Clarence, as he will do for his other projected murders. It is important that the audience be complicit in his villainy, that they admire his cleverness, that they are convinced that he keeps no secrets from them.

The sardonic sentiments of the soliloquy are realized in the next scene when Richard woos Lady Anne, who was married to King Henry VI's son Edward, whom Richard has killed, as well as the King himself. She calls him "thou lump of foul deformity" (1.2.57) and "hedgehog" (102); after she spits on him, she says: "Never hung poison on a fouler toad" (147). But Richard wins Anne by claiming that her beauty was the motive for all the murders:

Your beauty, that did haunt me in my sleep
To undertake the death of all the world,
So I might live one hour in your sweet bosom. (122–24)

After she has been won, Anne says "I would I knew thy heart" (193), but Richard is as inscrutable as Iago. Both offer no explanations for their actions, except to the audience in their abundant soliloquies, and that is very practical and matter of fact.

When Anne has exited, Richard has only contempt and disdain for her foolish agreement to be his wife:

Was ever woman in this humor wooed?
Was ever woman in this humor won?
I'll have her, but I will not keep her long.
What! I that killed her husband and his father
To take her in her heart's extremest hate.
With curses in her mouth, tears in her eyes,
The bleeding witness of my hatred by,
Having God, her conscience, and these bars against me,
And I no friends to back my suit at all
But the plain devil and dissembling looks,
And yet to win her, all the world to nothing!
Ha! (227–38)

The meaningless expletive "Ha," a word closely associated with Iago, expresses Richard's astonishment at his success with Anne. He is proud of his skill as a rhetorician, in the root sense of language meant to persuade. But he already anticipates Anne's death—"I will not keep her long." These comments have nothing to do with love, but only with Richard's misogyny coupled with his soaring ambition.

He is indignant at her heartlessness, as if he himself were speaking as a moral, Christian citizen:

> Hath she forgot already that brave prince,
> Edward her lord, whom I, some three months since,
> Stabbed in my angry mood at Tewkesbury?
> A sweeter and a lovelier gentleman,
> Framed in the prodigality of nature,
> Young, valiant, wise, and, no doubt, right royal,
> The spacious world cannot again afford.
> And will she yet abase her eyes on me,
> That cropped the golden prime of this sweet prince
> And made her widow to a woeful bed?
> On me, whose all not equals Edward's moi'ty [half]?
> On me, that halts and am misshapen thus? (239–50)

This is Richard at his most sardonic, enjoying the enormity of his crimes. One could ask: if Edward were all of these beautiful things, then why did Richard kill him? Richard makes no attempt at all to justify the murders, except that he did all this for the far-fetched reason of his overwhelming love for Anne.

Notice how quickly he reverts to his own deformity, which he suddenly turns around to its opposite:

> My dukedom to a beggarly denier [small coin],
> I do mistake my person all this while.
> Upon my life, she finds, although I cannot,
> Myself to be a marv'lous proper [handsome] man.
> I'll be at charges for a looking glass
> And entertain a score or two of tailors
> To study fashions to adorn my body.
> Since I am crept in favor with myself,
> I will maintain it with some little cost. (251–59)

Of course, Richard doesn't plan to do any of these things. He is just having a good time at the expense of Anne's foolish and mistaken judgment. He ends the scene with a ringing couplet:

> Shine out, fair sun, till I have bought a glass
> That I may see my shadow as I pass. (262–63)

The glass or mirror functions as a very important symbol for self-examination, as in *Richard II* (4.1.264) or in a work like *A Mirror for Magistrates* (1559), but in this context it has only a superficial, ironic meaning.

The wooing of Anne in Act I, scene ii is recapitulated in Act IV, scene iv, when Richard solicits his brother Edward's Queen Elizabeth to woo her daughter Elizabeth for him. It is an excessively long and tedious scene because Richard's protestations of love ring hollow. He exclaims again, as in his wooing of Anne, "that I did all this for love of her" (288), but Queen Elizabeth is not persuaded:

> Nay, then indeed she cannot choose but hate thee,
> Having bought love with such a bloody spoil. (289–90)

Richard cannot get around the fact that he has murdered Elizabeth's brothers, Edward and Richard. His talk of love is empty rhetoric.

Queen Elizabeth reminds him "thou didst kill my children" (422), so that Richard's elaborate poetizing has no effect:

> But in your daughter's womb I'll bury them,
> Where in that nest of spicery they will breed
> Selves of themselves, to your recomforture. (423–25)

In the phoenix myth the bird, returned to its nest made fragrant with spices, was consumed in fire, and from its ashes arose a new phoenix. It is a myth of rebirth and renewal. When Queen Elizabeth leaves, Richard has the same contempt for her that he had for Anne. He calls her "Relenting fool, and shallow, changing woman" (431), as if she will successfully woo her daughter for him, but instead Elizabeth marries Richmond, who will become King Henry VII.

There is a great deal of animal imagery for Richard as there is for many of Shakespeare's villains. It is a consistently negative imagery that allies the villain with the lowest forms of nature. Richard is linked with aggressive animals that bite, like the dog, the boar, the hedgehog, and the tiger; with venomous animals like the toad, the snake, the spider, and the lizard; and with mythical animals like the basilisk or cockatrice that kill merely by a look or by breathing on their victims.

Richard's heraldic emblem was the boar, which figures strongly in the play, especially in Act III, scene ii. A messenger reports to Hastings that Lord Stanley "dreamt the boar had rasèd off his helm" (11), in other words, that King Richard had cut off his head. Hastings will not flee with Stanley because

> To fly the boar before the boar pursues
> Were to incense the boar to follow us
> And make pursuit where he did mean no chase. (28–30)

Of course, Hastings is wrong and he is sent to his death in Act III, scene iv. We remember that in *Venus and Adonis* Adonis is killed by a boar.

Finally, in Richmond's heroic speech, Richard the boar is stigmatized as England's enemy; he is:

> The wretched, bloody, and usurping boar,
> That spoiled your summer fields and fruitful vines,
> Swills your warm blood like wash, and makes his trough
> In your emboweled bosoms, this foul swine
> Is now even in the center of this isle. . . . (5.2.7–11)

Richard the boar is represented as an ordinary hog, a "foul swine" intent on murder and pillage. It is clear that the boar will be destroyed and England returned to order by Henry Richmond.

The most frequent animal image for Richard is dog, cur, hell-hound. Queen Margaret addresses him as dog: "Stay, dog, for thou shalt hear me" (1.3.215), and curses him with vehemence:

> Thou elvish-marked, abortive, rooting hog!
> Thou that wast sealed in thy nativity
> The slave of nature and the son of hell! (1.3.227–29)

The hog is, of course, Richard's emblem (the boar). In Act IV, scene iv, Margaret continues her lamentations, this time accusing Richard's mother, the Duchess of York, in a violent dog imagery:

> From forth the kennel of thy womb hath crept
> A hellhound that doth hunt us all to death.
> That dog that had his teeth before his eyes
> To worry lambs and lap their gentle blood. . . .
> How do I thank thee that this carnal cur
> Preys on the issue of his mother's body. . . . (47–50, 56–57)

Richard is represented as a feral dog, a dog of prey. Queen Margaret hopes that she may "live and say, 'The dog is dead.'" (78). And this is precisely what Richmond says when he has killed Richard: "The day is ours; the bloody dog is dead" (5.5.2).

Richard is also represented by venomous, biting animals like the toad, the spider, and the lizard. They are all thought to be poisonous. Before Anne is won, she spits on him and says: "Never hung poison on a fouler toad" (1.2.147). Her next line is about Richard's eyes: "Would they were basilisks to strike thee dead!" (150). The basilisk, or cockatrice, was a mythical reptile whose look or breath was thought to kill. In IV.i Richard's mother laments that she has "hatched" a cockatrice "Whose unavoided eye is murderous" (54–55). Queen Margaret curses "this poisonous bunch-backed toad" (1.3.245). Richard's hump is seen to be filled with poison. Queen Elizabeth also calls him a "bunch-backed toad" (4.4.81) and his mother, the Duchess of York, continues the toad imagery when she asks her son: "Thou toad, thou toad, where is thy brother Clarence?" (145).

The references to toad are very similar to those to spider, which is also thought to be poisonous. Queen Margaret calls Richard a "bottled spider"(1.3.241). "Bottled," like "bunch-backed," alludes to Richard's hump; his back is represented as swollen because it is filled with poison. In Queen Elizabeth's curses, Richard is also a "bottled spider" (4.4.81). In *3 Henry VI* Queen Margaret confronts Richard with dire warnings. He is

like a foul misshapen stigmatic,
Marked by the Destinies to be avoided,
As venom toads, or lizards' dreadful stings. (2.2.136–38)

All of this negative imagery connects Richard's deformity with his diabolical and homicidal purposes. His misshapen body is an indication of his devilish origin. The animals link Richard with the forces of an aggressive and lacerating natural world. Despite his occasional professions of faith, Richard, like many of Shakespeare's villains, is an atheist and non-believer.

Also, like many of Shakespeare's villains, Richard is an excellent actor[3]— not only an actor but a comedian who delights in his villainy. I don't think that any of Shakespeare's villains, except for Macbeth, could be called tragic. They are busily engaged in role-playing, which is often joking and comic. In an aside in Act III, scene i, Richard identifies himself with the Vice of the morality plays:

Thus, like the formal Vice, Iniquity,
I moralize two meanings in one word. (3.1.82–83)

This is an important clue as to how Richard conceives his role. Already in *3 Henry VI*, before Richard kills the king, Henry addresses him as Roscius, the great Roman actor who died in 62 B.C.: "What scene of death hath Roscius now to act?" (5.6.10). This anticipates Hamlet's joking remark to Polonius: "My lord, I have news to tell you. When Roscius was an actor in Rome—" (*Hamlet* 2.2.399–400).

The most elaborately staged scenes are Act III, scene v and vii, when Richard contrives with Buckingham to be offered the crown by the Lord Mayor and the citizens of London, scenes that resemble Caesar's being offered the crown in *Julius Caesar* (I,ii). The opening stage direction in Act

III, scene v is: *"Enter Richard and Buckingham, in rotten armor, marvelous ill-favored."* This costume makes them seem humble. Richard begins the scene by asking Buckingham if he is ready for the acting exercise:

> Come, cousin, canst thou quake and change thy color,
> Murder thy breath in middle of a word,
> And then again begin, and stop again,
> As if thou wert distraught and mad with terror? (1–4)

Buckingham asserts that he is more than ready:

> Tut, I can counterfeit the deep tragedian,
> Speak and look back, and pry on every side,
> Tremble and start at wagging of a straw,
> Intending deep suspicion. (5–8)

Thus the histrionic strategy is in place for Richard to be crowned. Buckingham directs the scene in III,vii. Richard needs to

> get a prayer book in your hand
> And stand between two churchmen, good my lord,
> For on that ground I'll make a holy descant;
> And be not easily won to our requests.
> Play the maid's part: still answer nay, and take it. (46–50)

This strikingly anticipates the scene in *Hamlet* where Polonius stages Ophelia with a prayer book to encounter Hamlet:

> Read on this book,
> That show of such an exercise may color
> Your loneliness. We are oft to blame in this,
> 'Tis too much proved, that with devotion's visage
> And pious action we do sugar o'er
> The devil himself. (3.1.44–49)

Richard follows Buckingham's directions to the letter.

In the stage direction, we see Richard enter *"aloft, between two Bishops"* (3.7.93). Aloft is on the upper stage. Richard is very skillful in acting the reluctant "maid's part," although we are sure that even though he still answers nay, he is determined to "take it." He and Buckingham play wonderfully to each other, as if they have rehearsed their duet. Finally, Richard seems almost to agree to accept the crown:

Will you enforce me to a world of cares?
Call them again. I am not made of stone,
But penetrable to your kind entreaties,
Albeit against my conscience and my soul. (222–25)

The scene ends on a perfectly histrionic note. Richard says to the two Bishops that accompany him:

Come, let us to our holy work again.
Farewell, my cousin; farewell, gentle friends. (245–46)

The actors disperse and Richard prepares to kill Hastings. In the next scene (IV, ii), Buckingham falls out of favor and will soon be executed. In this scene, too, Richard is plotting the murder of his brother Edward's children in the Tower. As a counter-statement to his feigned humility in III,vii, he says:

But I am in
So far in blood that sin will pluck on sin.
Tear-falling pity dwells not in this eye. (4.2.62–64)

This anticipates Macbeth's frightening declaration as he prepares to kill Macduff's wife and children:

I am in blood
Stepped in so far that, should I wade no more,
Returning were as tedious as go o'er. (3.4.137–39)

Like Iago, Richard insists that he is an ordinary man, who protests strongly against the very politic devices and subtle stratagems that he himself uses. The irony is remarkable in his speech to Lord Grey, the son of Queen Elizabeth:

Because I cannot flatter and look fair,
Smile in men's faces, smooth, deceive, and cog [fawn],
Duck with French nods and apish courtesy,
I must be held a rancorous enemy.
Cannot a plain man live and think no harm
But thus his simple truth must be abused
With silken, sly, insinuating Jacks. (1.3.47–53)

But Richard is a rancorous enemy of Queen Elizabeth (who was Lady Grey), her brothers, and her children; he will soon dispose of them all.

In Act II, scene i, he makes a moving speech indicating that he desires "all good men's love" (62), concluding with a loving affirmation:

I do not know that Englishman alive
With whom my soul is any jot at odds
More than the infant that is born tonight.
I thank God for my humility. (71–73)

But the humble Richard ends up by killing or getting rid of most of the persons in this scene.

In a soliloquy in Act I, scene iii he makes a frank admission of his mode of operation:

But then I sigh, and with a piece of Scripture
Tell them that God bids us do good for evil;
And thus I clothe my naked villainy
With odd old ends stol'n forth of holy writ,
And seem a saint when most I play the devil. (333–37)

Notice that he plays the devil as if it were a dramatic role and he an actor. "Play' also indicates sport and a game to mark how much Richard is enjoying himself in his ruthless quest for the crown.

It's curious that the word "conscience" is used thirteen times in *Richard III* and has a special importance in this play (it occurs only eight times in *Hamlet*). In Queen Margaret's extensive curse in Act I, scene iii, she sets the terms for Richard's punishment:

The worm of conscience still begnaw thy soul!
Thy friends suspect for traitors while thou liv'st,
And take deep traitors for thy dearest friends! (221–23)

Conscience plays a part in Buckingham and Richard's arranged skit for making Richard king. It is all a prepared dialogue. When Richard hesitates, Buckingham says: "My lord, this argues conscience in your Grace" (3.7.173), and when Richard finally agrees to accept the crown, it is "against my conscience and my soul" (225). The interlude is well acted.

But by the end of the play, Richard's conscience really bothers him. When he *"starteth up out of a dream"*(5.3.177 s.d.), he speaks out of a deep despair and calls upon God:

Give me another horse! Bind up my wounds!
Have mercy, Jesu! Soft! I did but dream.
O coward conscience, how thou dost afflict me! (178–80)

This is continued in a long soliloquy about his guilt that resembles the soliloquy of Claudius in *Hamlet* (III, iii):

My conscience hath a thousand several tongues,
And every tongue brings in a several tale,
And every tale condemns me for a villain. (194–96)

Richard is acutely aware of his guilt: "I shall despair. There is no creature loves me" (201). Again, this is like the despair of Macbeth in V, iii and V, v. But, like Macbeth, Richard finally rejects the promptings of conscience:

Conscience is but a word that cowards use,
Devised at first to keep the strong in awe;
Our strong arms be our conscience, swords our law! (310–12)

So Richard ends by defying the pangs of conscience and fighting it out. At the very end he asserts that he has set his life "upon a cast" of the dice: "And I will stand the hazard of the die" (5.4.9–10). He is soon killed and Stanley cuts off his head:

Lo, here this long-usurpèd royalty
From the dead temples of this bloody wretch
Have I plucked off. . . . (5.5.4–6)

Notice that Richard appeals not to God but to chance, a role of the dice, "the hazard of the die," to survive, as the suitors of Portia in *The Merchant of Venice* hazard all on the three caskets (II,vii and ix). It is obvious that Richard the villain cannot survive the beneficent forces of Richmond.

Richard, Duke of Gloucester (who later becomes King Richard III), is Shakespeare's most notable creation to date. He is featured in two plays, *3 Henry VI* and *Richard III*, and he also appears in *2 Henry VI*. In his vaunting and ruthless ambition he resembles Marlowe's Tamburlaine of less than ten years earlier. Richard is preoccupied with his own deformity, as if this insures him of a special place among Shakespeare's protagonists. Albeit evil, he is a character of tremendous energy and imagination. Like Buckingham, he can "counterfeit the deep tragedian" (*Richard III* 3.5.5) and play whatever roles are necessary to accomplish his nefarious purposes. He is tricky and unpredictable, except that we know that he plans to murder everyone who stands in his way of becoming king. He definitely looks forward to Macbeth, who is a hero-villain in an entirely different mode but equally steeped in blood.

NOTES

1. Robert Ornstein has an eloquent and surprisingly sympathetic defense of Richard in *A Kingdom for a Stage: The Achievement of Shakespeare's History Plays*, Cambridge, MA: Harvard University Press, 1972. Reprinted in the Signet edition of *Richard III*,

ed. Mark Eccles, New York, 1988. For an excellent close reading of the play see Wolfgang Clemen, *A Commentary on Shakespeare's Richard III*, tr. Jean Bonheim, London, 1968. First published in 1957.

2. See the interesting equation of deformity and depravity in this play in Paul V. Kreider, *Repetition in Shakespeare's Plays*, Princeton, NJ: Princeton University Press, 1941, p.55. About half this book is on Shakespeare's villains.

3. Antony Hammond, in his Arden edition of *King Richard III* (London, 1981), takes thorough account of Richard's relation to the Vice figure—always very histrionic—of the morality plays, pp. 99–103, and also to the Renaissance Machiavel (pp. 104–5). Cf. Bernard Spevack, *Shakespeare and the Allegory of Evil*, New York, NY: Columbia University Press, 1958. There is an excellent account of the role-playing of Richard in Peter Ure, "Character and Role from *Richard III* to *Hamlet*," in *Elizabethan and Jacobean Drama: Critical Essays by Peter Ure*, ed. J. C. Maxwell, Liverpool, UK: Liverpool University Press, 1974, Ch. 2. Ure says teasingly that Richard "can no longer engage in his characteristic pleasurable activity, and play the part of king with his usual merrily critical detachment, when he is the king" (p. 28). See also Thomas F. Van Laan, *Role-playing in Shakespeare*, Toronto, ON: University of Toronto Press, 1978.

Chapter 4

Shylock

Shylock appears in a comedy, but he has a much smaller role to play than Richard III, Aaron, or Iago, who dominate their plays. In *The Merchant of Venice* the Venetian action is set against the action in Belmont, and Shylock disappears from the play at the end of Act IV. Shylock is never really a comic figure, but rather grotesque and sardonic, set apart from the other characters because he is an alien. On Shakespeare's stage, from what we know, he was probably costumed as identifiably Jewish, in a long gabardine cloak, with a red beard and wig (to emphasize his resemblance to Judas) and a putty nose—what we would think of as a clown's outfit. But he is a sinister figure, joking and insulting at the same time, and sardonically exposing the hypocrisies of the Venetians. He is sympathetic only because he is so obviously victimized by his Christian compatriots. If Shylock is a villain, then Shakespeare goes to a great deal of trouble to defend him—much more trouble than he takes with other villains.

But he is, of course, a significant villain. One of the basic ways to define a villain in Shakespeare is: someone willing to kill to gain his ends. In the trial scene (IV, i), Bassanio asks: "Do all men kill the things they do not love?" to which the relentless Shylock answers: "Hates any man the thing he would not kill?" (66–67). This is a crucial statement. Bassanio seems shocked by Shylock's unmitigated homicidal intent. He tries to reason with him on Antonio's behalf: "Every offense is not a hate at first," but Shylock's hatred cannot be touched by reason: "What, wouldst thou have a serpent sting thee twice?" (68–69). This is a joking answer in Shylock's characteristic sardonic style. A poisonous serpent needs to sting only once.

There is a great deal of animal imagery for Shylock, as there is for many of Shakespeare's villains. The dog (cur) image is the most frequent, as it is for Richard III and Iago. Shylock seems to take special pleasure in describing his abased status as a Jew in Venice. With Antonio, the venture capitalist who comes for a loan, Shylock is sardonic in a provocative way. He reminds Antonio of his gross anti-Semitism:

> You call me misbeliever, cutthroat dog,
> And spet upon my Jewish gabardine. . . . (1.3.108–9)

He mocks Antonio's pleading tone:

> You come to me and you say,
> "Shylock, we would have moneys"—you say so,
> You that did void your rheum upon my beard
> And foot me as you spurn a stranger cur
> Over your threshold! (112–16)

Shylock is at his ease here and positively expansive as he speculates in what voice he should answer Antonio's suit:

> Moneys is your suit.
> What should I say to you? Should I not say
> "Hath a dog money? Is it possible
> A cur can lend three thousand ducats?" (116–19)

He continues the dialogue with obvious satisfaction:

> Fair sir, you spet on me on Wednesday last,
> You spurned me such a day, another time
> You called me dog; and for these courtesies
> I'll lend you thus much moneys? (123–26)

The irony is heavy.

In Act III, scene iii, the dog images become more dire as Shylock addresses Antonio:

> I have sworn an oath that I will have my bond.
> Thou call'dst me dog before thou hadst a cause,
> But since I am a dog, beware my fangs. (5–7)

"Fangs," of course, usually belong to serpents, but Shylock is using the same biting imagery as Richard, Duke of Gloucester. He is on the attack with dog and animal imagery in the trial scene (IV,i), when he reminds the Duke that Venice is a slave-holding society:

> You have among you many a purchased slave,
> Which like your asses and your dogs and mules
> You use in abject and in slavish parts,
> Because you bought them. (90–93)

Again, Shylock mocks the Venetians by imitating his own hypothetical speech:

> Shall I say to you,
> "Let them be free! Marry them to your heirs!
> Why sweat they under burdens? Let their beds
> Be made as soft as yours, and let their palates
> Be seasoned with such viands"? (93–97)

It seems as if he delights to play the clown in order to drive home his satiric points.

Shylock's enemies use the same dog and animal imagery to insult him as a worthless, debased Jew, beginning with Solanio, who calls him "the dog Jew" (2.8.14) and "the most impenetrable cur/ That ever kept with men" (3.3.18–19). But Gratiano develops this imagery most fully. In the trial scene he calls Shylock an "inexecrable dog" (128) and goes on to offer a Pythagorean theory of the transmigration of souls:

> Thou almost mak'st me waver in my faith,
> To hold opinion with Pythagoras
> That souls of animals infuse themselves
> Into the trunks of men. Thy currish spirit
> Governed a wolf who, hanged for human slaughter,
> Even from the gallows did his fell [fierce] soul fleet,
> And whilst thou layest in thy unhallowed dam,
> Infused itself in thee; for thy desires
> Are wolvish, bloody, starved, and ravenous. (130–38)

It is useful to have this strange speech of Gratiano in order to establish the degree of Venetian hatred of Shylock unleashed in the trial scene.

Shylock's food and eating imagery has a similar negative tone to the animal imagery. Since Shylock is Jewish and keeps kosher, he has a particular animus against eating with Christians. He answers Bassanio's invitation to dine with a vehement denunciation:

Yes, to smell pork, to eat of the habitation which your prophet the Naza-
rite [Christ] conjured the devil into! I will buy with you, sell with you, talk
with you, walk with you, and so following; but I will not eat with you, drink
with you, nor pray with you. (1.3.31–35)

It is ironic that in Shylock's very sympathetic speech in this scene ("Hath not
a Jew eyes?") he claims that Jews and Christians are "fed with the same food"
(57–58). Of course they are not—remember that Shylock keeps kosher—and
food images have a special negative meaning for him.

Throughout the eating imagery (which relates to the pound of flesh bond),
there is a strong cannibalistic note, as in Shylock's comments in an aside,
when he first sees Antonio:

If I can catch him once upon the hip,
I will feed fat the ancient grudge I bear him. (43–44)

To catch upon the hip is a term from wrestling meaning to catch at a disadvan-
tage, but there is probably an allusion to Jacob's wrestling with an angel in *Gen-
esis* 32, since Shylock's thinking is steeped in the Old Testament. To "feed fat"
is to feed excessively so that one becomes fat. It is a dire prediction of Shylock's
using his "merry bond" to take Antonio's life, literally to eat him up.

This seems to be what Shylock is thinking about at the end of the scene,
when he speaks of the pound of flesh along with other meats that are eaten
for dinner:

If he should break his day, what should I gain
By the exaction of the forfeiture?
A pound of man's flesh taken from a man
Is not so estimable, profitable neither,
As flesh of muttons, beefs, or goats. (160–64)

What Shylock means by "estimable" and "profitable" is edible and tasty. This
is scary.

In Act II, scene v Shylock does go to supper with his Christian clients, but
he makes it clear to Jessica that he goes reluctantly:

I am not bid for love—they flatter me.
But yet I'll go in hate, to feed upon
The prodigal Christian. (13–15)

Shylock is thrifty but the Christian is prodigal or wasteful. Again, we have
a cannibalistic image for Shylock, who thinks of eating as an aggressive act
of devouring one's enemies. His revenge is represented in terms of eating. In

answer to Salerio's question: "Why, I am sure if he forfeit thou wilt not take his flesh. What's that good for?" (3.1.48–49), Shylock is very specific about his homicidal intent: "To bait fish withal. If it will feed nothing else, if will feed my revenge" (50–51). So feeding is established in the play as an actively aggressive term, like the feeding of an animal.

Like other Shakespearean villains, Shylock shows his derivation from the Vice figure of the medieval moralities by his dark jocularity. His style is full of odd mannerisms, for example when he first appears in the play at Act I, scene iii. In his opening exchanges with Bassanio he says only: "Three thousand ducats—well" (1), "For three months—well" (3), and "Antonio shall become bound—well" (6). Those three "well's" are ominous, as if Shylock is determined to say nothing except for a kind of repetitious humming. The fourth exchange is also blank: "Three thousand ducats for three months, and Antonio bound" (9–10), as is the fifth: "Antonio is a good man" (12). Then Shylock launches into a long, wordy speech ending with an outrageous pun:

> But ships are but boards, sailors but men; there be land rats and water rats, water thieves and land thieves—I mean pirates. . . . (21–24)

Bassanio is not amused by Shylock's primitive wordplay ("pie-rats"). There is another bitter pun in Act III, scene i, when Solanio makes fun of Jessica's flight, something Shylock takes with deadly seriousness:

> *Solanio.* And Shylock for his own part knew the bird was fledge [feathered], and then it is the complexion of them all to leave the dam [mother].
> *Shylock.* She is damned for it. (27–30)

Shylock's murderous bond is represented perversely as a "merry bond" (1.3.170). It is here that the black comedy of the play is most in evidence, since, on the surface, Shylock pretends that he is showing Antonio much "kindness" (140) in not charging him interest. It is all done in a spirit of "merry sport" (142), and the word "sport," favored by Aaron and Iago, has strong connotations of the villain as jester. It is a merry sport because it is so unlikely that the wealthy Antonio will default. Shylock must speak these lines in an amused and light-hearted tone:

> let the forfeit
> Be nominated for an equal pound
> Of your fair flesh, to be cut off and taken
> In what part of your body pleaseth me. (145–48)

At this point Shylock seems whimsical. He doesn't say anything about cutting the pound of Antonio's "fair flesh" from his heart, but only from "what part of your body pleaseth me." Antonio is not yet the unimaginable victim.

In Shylock's most sympathetic speech in the play ("Hath not a Jew eyes?"), some of the statements are bizarrely unanticipated, such as his question: "If you tickle us, do we not laugh?" (3.1.61–62). Why is Shylock talking about such a childish manipulation as tickling and its subsequent laughter in such a serious passage setting forth the common humanity that Christians and Jews share? But in its immediate context Shylock's sardonic and homicidal mood is abundantly evident:

> If you prick us, do we not bleed? If you tickle us, do we not laugh? If you poison
> us, do we not die? And if you wrong us, shall we not revenge? (61–63)

Shylock moves quickly and without transition from pricking, bleeding, tickling, and laughing to poisoning and revenge.

In the trial scene (IV,i) Shylock is on a triumphant high because he is sure that his bond is tamper-proof, that he is protected by "commodity" (3.3.27)— the profitable laws of commerce in Venice. This the same as the Bastard's "tickling commodity,/ Commodity, the bias of the world" in *King John* (2.1.573–74). It is expediency for profit. That is why, in answering the Duke, Shylock feels he can indulge his savage jocularity:

> You'll ask me why I rather choose to have
> A weight of carrion flesh than to receive
> Three thousand ducats. I'll not answer that,
> But say it is my humor. (4.1.40–43)

"Humor" is a physiological term derived from the medieval doctrine of the four humors, but here it means whim or caprice. This is like T. S. Eliot's discussion of Marlowe's *The Jew of Malta* as "the farce of the old English humour, the terribly serious, even savage comic humour, the humour which spent its last breath in the decadent genius of Dickens."[1]

Shylock demonstrates his "humor" by providing the Duke with absurd examples of a non-explanation:

> What if my house be troubled with a rat,
> And I be pleased to give ten thousand ducats
> To have it baned [poisoned]? (44–46)

Ten thousand ducats, more than three times the amount of the bond, is a pre-
posterous sum, but Shylock is toying with the Duke: "What, are you answered
yet" (46)? This is followed by a string of equally ridiculous examples:

> Some men there are love not a gaping pig,
> Some that are mad if they behold a cat,
> And others, when the bagpipe sings i' th' nose,
> Cannot contain their urine. . . . (47–50)

Maybe it is not so absurd that the aging Shylock is afraid of urinary
incontinence.

Shylock attributes all of his capricious examples to the force of "affection,/
Master of passion" (50–51), or, in other words, to his personal inclinations.
But he acknowledges that this is a non-explanation:

> So can I give no reason, nor I will not,
> More than a lodged hate and a certain loathing
> I bear Antonio, that I follow thus
> A losing suit against him. Are you answered? (59–62)

A bit further on we see him whetting his knife on the sole of his shoe (121).

Shylock is not a villain-hero like Macbeth, but there is an essential ambiguity
in his character. There is no doubt that he is a villain,[2] like many other villains
in Shakespeare. Yet he is also in many ways very sympathetic. His heartfelt
speech, "Hath not a Jew eyes?" (3.1.55–56), is the most moving, humanistic
declaration that any Jew speaks in all of Elizabethan/Jacobean drama. There
is nothing at all like it in Marlowe's play, *The Jew of Malta* (produced about
1592), which serves as a model for *The Merchant of Venice.* Also, Shylock is
seen to be victimized by Christian society in Venice, especially by Antonio.

As it turns out, the polite and gracious Antonio is a violent anti-Semite,
who is the source of many of the insults and spurning actions that Shylock
mentions. There is a deliberate matching of the two men. For example, Shylock says:

> You call me misbeliever, cutthroat dog,
> And spet upon my Jewish gabardine,
> And all for use of that which is mine own. (1.3.108–10)

Antonio answers, using the same imagery:

> I am as like to call thee so again,
> To spet on thee again, to spurn thee too.

If thou wilt lend this money, lend it not
As to thy friends . . .
But lend it rather to thine enemy. (127–30, 132)

Shylock manages to bait the seemingly imperturbable, generous, charitable Christian gentleman Antonio. The loan is immediately set in a context of hate, viciousness, and dire forebodings.

When his daughter Jessica abandons him and elopes with Lorenzo, Shylock changes significantly. He is now enraged and no longer playfully jesting about his merry bond. Jessica not only flees from her father's house and converts to Christianity, but she also brazenly steals her father's money and many valuable jewels. One particular item figures into the account given by Tubal, a fellow Jew, of Jessica and her new husband's living it up—like Bonnie and Clyde—with Shylock's stolen wealth in Genoa. Jessica suddenly becomes an extravagant young woman, ridiculously spendthrift, as Tubal reports: "Your daughter spent in Genoa, as I heard, one night fourscore ducats" (3.1.101–2). English audiences would not know exactly what the ducat was worth, but fourscore seems like an exceedingly large sum. Shylock cries out in what seems like physical pain: "Thou stick'st a dagger in me. I shall never see my gold again. Fourscore ducats at a sitting, fourscore ducats!" (103–5). Shylock cannot believe what he is hearing. The crowning blow is Tubal's report that one of Antonio's creditors "showed me a ring that he had of your daughter for a monkey" (111–12). This is the last straw for the already exasperated father:

> Out upon her! Thou torturest me, Tubal. It was my turquoise; I had it of Leah
> when I was a bachelor. I would not have given it for a wilderness of monkeys.
> (113–16)

This is the first—and last—we hear of Shylock's deceased wife Leah, who presented him with the very turquoise ring that his daughter has now so foolishly traded for a monkey. This is an utterly contemptuous transaction, which might inspire a comment like that of King Lear on his daughter Goneril: "How sharper than a serpent's tooth it is/ To have a thankless child" (1.4.295–96). But Shylock expresses his boundless rage in a curious commercial image: "I would not have given it for a wilderness of monkeys" (115–16). In other words, his daughter is not only insulting the memory of her mother, but she is also totally unaware of the ring's market value. Admittedly, the turquoise, or "turkey stone," is only a semi-precious jewel, but it has a powerful sentimental worth. It is at this point that Shylock is monomaniacally set on revenge as a satisfaction for his lost daughter: "I will have the heart of him if he forfeit" (120). It is no longer a merry bond in which Shylock will hypothetically demand

an equal pound
Of your fair flesh, to be cut off and taken
In what part of your body pleaseth me. (1.3.146–48)

Shylock now will only settle for cutting out Antonio's heart.

In the trial scene (IV,i) he cleverly attacks the Duke and the magnificoes of Venice as sponsors of a slave-holding society. This is a way of balancing his thirst for revenge with the hypocrisy on which Venetian society is founded. With obvious pleasure, Shylock reminds the Duke:

What judgment shall I dread, doing no wrong?
You have among you many a purchased slave,
Which like your asses and your dogs and mules
You use in abject and in slavish parts,
Because you bought them. Shall I say to you,
"Let them be free! Marry them to your heirs!
Why sweat they under burdens? Let their beds
Be made as soft as yours, and let their palates
Be seasoned with such viands"? (4.1.89–97)

Shakespeare must be thinking of Marlowe's play, *The Jew of Malta*, where Barabas buys Ithamore at a slave auction.

We are back at the sardonic Shylock of the earlier scenes, teasing the smug and moralistic Venetians with malicious irony. He puts words in their mouth:

You will answer,
"The slaves are ours." So do I answer you:
The pound of flesh which I demand of him
Is dearly bought, is mine, and I will have it.
If you deny me, fie upon your law!
There is no force in the decrees of Venice.
I stand for judgment. Answer; shall I have it? (97–103)

For "dearly bought" we remember Portia's commercial image for Bassanio: "Since you are dear bought, I will love you dear" (3.2.313).

Venice is an international trading center that depends upon the rule of law. Antonio, who is himself a venture capitalist in shipping, knows exactly why he is doomed:

The Duke cannot deny the course of law;
For the commodity that strangers [foreigners] have
With us in Venice, if it be denied,
Will much impeach the justice of the state,

Since that the trade and profit of the city
Consisteth of all nations. (3.3.26–31)

So Shylock is riding high in the trial scene without any doubt that the laws
of Venice will honor his bond, which is, after all, a legitimate commercial
contract.

This is the high point of Shylock's folly. When Nerissa, Portia's waiting
gentlewoman, enters disguised as a law clerk, he makes an unforgettable
stage gesture: he whets his knife on the sole of his shoe, the very knife with
which he intends to cut the pound of flesh from Antonio's heart. Bassanio
calls attention to the stage business: "Why dost thou whet thy knife so ear-
nestly" (121)? Shylock answers without any apologies: "To cut the forfeiture
from that bankrout there" (122). Gratiano makes the obvious pun:

Not on thy sole, but on thy soul, harsh Jew,
Thou mak'st thy knife keen; but no metal can—
No, not the hangman's ax—bear half the keenness
Of thy sharp envy [malice]. (123–26)

Of course, we are not going to allow Shylock, the Jewish money lender, to
savagely murder Antonio, the Christian capitalist, right on stage before our
eyes. Portia soon enters, disguised as Balthasar, a young Doctor of Laws,
and Shylock is undone by a legal technicality: his bond calls for a pound of
flesh—exactly one pound—and not a single drop of blood. Portia drives the
point home with a self-congratulatory legalism:

If thou tak'st more
Or less than a just pound, be it but so much
As makes it light or heavy in the substance
Or the division of the twentieth part
Of one poor scruple—nay, if the scale do turn
But in the estimation [value] of a hair—
Thou diest, and all thy goods are confiscate. (325–31)

Portia eagerly presses on with her legal subterfuge without much concern for
the "quality of mercy" (183) she asks from Shylock. He is totally humiliated
and crushed. Before he leaves the stage, he agrees to surrender his estate
and convert to Christianity. He exits never to reappear, making the fifth act,
despite its big lyric set pieces on the power of music and its catalogue of for-
saken lovers, anticlimactic. The play is never able to recover its comic tone.

Shylock is destroyed by the very legality he has had so much faith in. Like
Othello, he is suddenly made aware of what he has tacitly known all along:
that he is an alien in the state of Venice without the rights that belong to a

Venetian citizen. Portia delights in rubbing it in, and again we feel a strong current of anti-Semitism:

Tarry, Jew!
The law hath yet another hold on you.
It is enacted in the laws of Venice,
If it be proved against an alien
That by direct or indirect attempts
He seek the life of any citizen,
The party 'gainst the which he doth contrive
Shall seize one half his goods; the other half
Comes to the privy coffer of the state;
And the offender's life lies in the mercy
Of the Duke. . . . (345–55)

Portia's key word "mercy" is used ironically in the rest of this scene as the Duke spares Shylock's life and makes what he considers a just and merciful seizure of his goods. It is suddenly brought home to Shylock, as it is to Othello, that there is one set of laws for citizens of Venice and another for aliens.

So which is the real Shylock? I think that this is a question that Shakespeare never allows us to answer. James Shapiro's book, *Shakespeare and the Jews*, enters the debate by broadening the topic of the status of Jews in England just before the date of Shakespeare's play in the 1590's and just after.[3] *The Merchant of Venice* is intended to give comfort to neither philo-Semitic nor anti-Semitic audiences or readers. We are forced to remain with the paradox that Shylock is the most sympathetic and highly characterized Jew in Shakespeare and in all of Elizabethan/Jacobean drama, but he is also a fierce and savage killer, intent on extracting a monomaniacal revenge for real and imagined wrongs. He doesn't seem to love anyone, not Tubal, not his daughter, and probably not even his long dead wife Leah. Yet he forces us to have compassion for him not so much as a Jew but as a persecuted human being.

NOTES

1. T. S. Eliot. "Christopher Marlowe," *Selected Essays 1917–1932*, New York, NY, 1932, p. 105.

2. John Russell Brown, in his Arden edition of *The Merchant of Venice* (London, 1955), speaks eloquently of Shylock as a villain in pp. xxxvii–xlv of the introduction. See also Maurice Charney, "Shylock as Villain," *Shakespeare Newsletter*, 59 (2009–2010), 85–86, 88, 100.

3. James Shapiro. *Shakespeare and the Jews*, New York, NY: Columbia University Press, 1996.

Chapter 5

Claudius

Claudius is different from other Shakespearean villains we have discussed.[1]
He is not jocular or sardonic like Aaron, Richard Duke of Gloucester, Iago, or
Shylock, but like them he is a killer. I think that this is an element that connects all of Shakespeare's villains. Polonius is linked with Claudius because,
presumably, he helps him to the throne. Under Claudius we may also include
Rosencrantz and Guildenstern, his dutiful spies, who extend his role as villain. Polonius, Rosencrantz, and Guildenstern are not villains in their own
right, but they are tools of the King.

Claudius is a secret villain, and this may explain why the role of soliloquy
and aside is less significant in *Hamlet* than it is in *Othello* or in *3 Henry VI*
and *Richard III*. Claudius has a long soliloquy in Act III, scene iii, a short
soliloquy at the end of Act IV, scene iii, and two brief asides, but he doesn't
need the complicity of the audience as Iago and Richard Duke of Gloucester
do. They take the audience into their confidence and share their secrets with
them, but Claudius has a different relation to the audience. He is deceptive
and indulges in false appearances. Right after the Ghost has told him about
his secret murder, Hamlet expresses his new vision of his uncle:

O villain, villain, smiling, damnèd villain!
My tables [notebook]—meet it is I set it down
That one may smile, and smile, and be a villain.
At least I am sure it may be so in Denmark. (1.5.106–9)

Claudius's first speech in the play already identifies him, stylistically, as a
"smiling villain." His address to the court of Denmark is very rhetorical, with

55

long, polysyllabic sentences that remind us of Polonius's more exaggerated "art"—remember how impatient the Queen is with Polonius's circumlocution: "More matter, with less art" (2.2.95). In Act I, scene ii, the King delivers a public oration, displaying his skill at showy (or what we think of as banal) metaphor. He has married the Queen

> as 'twere, with a defeated joy,
> With an auspicious and a dropping eye,
> With mirth in funeral, and with dirge in marriage,
> In equal scale weighing delight and dole. . . . (10–13)

The King luxuriates in his elaborate figure of speech. He then dispatches business of state. He minimizes the threat of "young Fortinbras," who "hath not failed to pester us with message" (22). The King dismisses him with imperious brevity: "So much for him" (25). So we already see another side to Claudius's long-windedness.

With Laertes the King is much more unctuously flattering, since he is the son of Polonius, his chief counselor of state, and presumably the person who has helped him to the throne. The King dwells lovingly on Laertes's name, as if he were stroking him:

> And now, Laertes, what's the news with you?
> You told us of some suit. What is't, Laertes?
> You cannot speak of reason to the Dane
> And lose your voice. What wouldst thou beg, Laertes,
> That shall not be my offer, not thy asking?
> The head is not more native to the heart,
> The hand more instrumental to the mouth,
> Than is the throne of Denmark to thy father.
> What wouldst thou have, Laertes? (42–50)

The King, of course, agrees at once with Laertes's desire to return to France.

With Hamlet, the King speaks entirely differently. He ignores his bitter asides and the fact that Hamlet's speech is mostly directed to his mother. He lectures his son (step-son) in the same platitudinous terms as his first speech in the scene. It is "sweet and commendable" in Hamlet's nature to mourn for his father, but he should know

> your father lost a father,
> That father lost, lost his, and the survivor bound
> In filial obligation for some term
> To do obsequious sorrow. But to persever

In obstinate condolement is a course
Of impious stubbornness. (89–94)

Again, Claudius is playing the orator, with latinate, polysyllabic moralizing.
But, with excessively elaborate courtesy, he refuses Hamlet's request to go
back to school in Wittenberg:

And we beseech you, bend you to remain
Here in the cheer and comfort of our eye,
Our chiefest courtier, cousin, and our son. (115–17)

Hamlet is not much impressed with this shallow flattery. He does not
answer the King and addresses himself only to his mother: "I shall in all my
best obey you, madam" (120). Claudius's answer is surprising because it
totally ignores the import of what Hamlet has said:

Why, 'tis a loving and a fair reply.
Be as ourself in Denmark. Madam, come.
This gentle and unforced accord of Hamlet
Sits smiling to my heart. . . . (121–24)

Of course, it is not at all a loving and a fair reply, nor does Hamlet extend a
gentle and unforced accord. In a few moments he launches into his bitter and
disillusioned soliloquy: "O that this too too sullied flesh would melt" (129).

The King's aside in Act III, scene i is crucial to our understanding of his
villainous role. In context, the aside occurs right after Polonius has set up his
daughter to confront Hamlet as a test whether he is mad for her love. Polonius
and the King will hide as "lawful espials" (32). Polonius directs Ophelia, as
if she were a beginning actress, to read on a book, presumably a book of religious devotions, "That show of such an exercise may color [disguise]/ Your
loneliness [aloneness]" (45–46).

It is Polonius's moral commentary that directly triggers Claudius's aside:

We are oft to blame in this,
'Tis too much proved, that with devotion's visage
And pious action we do sugar o'er
The devil himself. (46–49)

Claudius responds directly and literally to Polonius's remarks:

O, 'tis too true.
How smart a lash that speech doth give my conscience!
The harlot's cheek, beautied with plast'ring art,
Is not more ugly to the thing that helps it

Than is my deed to my most painted word.
O heavy burden! (49–54)

It is crucial to the narrative that we hear about Claudius's guilt *before* the *Mousetrap* play, in which Hamlet vows to "catch the conscience of the King" (2.2.617). The King's aside in Act III, scene i makes it clear that his conscience is already caught by Polonius's moral observations.

What the King says about the hypocritical, false appearances presented by cosmetics is repeated some hundred lines further in Hamlet's confrontation with Ophelia: "I have heard of your paintings, well enough. God hath given you one face, and you make yourselves another" (144–46). The harlot, beautified by "plast'ring art" or face painting, was a familiar symbol of deception. Claudius's "painted word," or art of rhetoric, is contrasted with his deeds, a theme more fully developed in the King's long soliloquy in Act III, scene iii.

"Conscience" is a critical word in this play. Hamlet uses it four times, and once, crucially, in his "To be, or not to be" soliloquy, just 33 lines after Claudius's aside: "Thus conscience does make cowards of us all" (83), as if he were echoing the smart lash that conscience gives the King. Claudius uses "conscience" only once more, when he is tricking Laertes into the triple plot against Hamlet:

Now must your conscience my acquittance seal,
And you must put me in your heart for friend,
Sith you have heard, and with a knowing ear,
That he which hath your noble father slain
Pursued my life. (4.7.1–5)

Of course, this is false, but Laertes is easily persuaded to kill for revenge. In an earlier scene, he wished "Conscience and grace to the profoundest pit!/ I dare damnation" (4.5.132–33). At the very end of the play, he appears to be repentant; he vows to hit Hamlet, but he adds in an aside: "And yet it is almost against my conscience" (5.2.297). Shakespeare makes a strenuous effort to rehabilitate Laertes and to separate him from Claudius's villainy.

Claudius's long soliloquy in Act III, scene iii essentially continues his aside and the pricking of his conscience. This is the most sympathetic moment for the King in the play, like Shylock's "Hath not a Jew eyes?" speech in *The Merchant of Venice* (3.1.56ff). Claudius is powerfully aware that his "offense is rank" (3.3.36), like Cain's murder of his brother Abel. One meaning of "rank" is stinking. In this soliloquy the King shows himself to be painfully conscious of his guilt in the eyes of heaven, even if he has been successful in covering up his crime:

In the corrupted currents of this world
Offense's gilded hand may shove by justice,
And oft 'tis seen the wicked prize itself

Buys out the law. But 'tis not so above.
There is no shuffling. . . . (57–60)

"Shuffling" is a graphic word, referring literally to a shuffling or shambling gait, but it is also a term from cards, implying trickery in shuffling the deck. Meaning 7 of "shuffle" in the *Oxford English Dictionary* summarizes its consistently negative connotations: "To act in a shifting or evasive manner; to shift one's ground in argument, etc.; to make use of deceitful pretences or shifty answers." Thus in the plot against Hamlet, Claudius advises Laertes that Hamlet

being remiss,
Most generous, and free from all contriving,
Will not peruse the foils, so that with ease,
Or with a little shuffling, you may choose
A sword unbated, and, in a pass of practice [a treacherous thrust],
Requite him for your father. (4.7.134–39)

This is the kind of shuffling that Claudius is certain cannot exist in the judgment of heaven.

He is enough of a theologian to know that there is no possibility that his prayer may be answered. Clearly, since one cannot "be pardoned and retain th' offense" (3.3.56), no kind of prayer will serve:

"Forgive me my foul murder"?
That cannot be, since I am still possessed
Of those effects for which I did the murder,
My crown, mine own ambition, and my queen. (52–55)

It is remarkable how profoundly Claudius understands the Christian doctrine of grace: God's mercy is infinite, there is no sin that cannot be forgiven, except that the sinner has to be truly penitent. It is pretty much the same argument as at the end of Marlowe's *Doctor Faustus*. Salvation is open to all, but not to an unrepentant King Claudius or Doctor Faustus.

In Claudius's next soliloquy (at the end of Act IV, scene iii), there is no longer any talk of prayer or repentance. We see him once more as a cold-blooded murderer planning Hamlet's death:

And, England, if my love thou hold'st at aught . . .
thou may'st not coldly set
Our sovereign process, which imports at full
By letters congruing to that effect
The present death of Hamlet. Do it, England,

For like the hectic in my blood he rages,
And thou must cure me. (58, 62–67)

"Hectic" is a strong word for a consumptive fever, its only use in Shakespeare.
We are made to feel Claudius's overpowering homicidal mood. Hamlet's
murder is the only thing that can cure the "hectic" in the King's blood.

Incidentally, we get some further details about Claudius's "grand commission" (5.2.18) to have his step-son murdered from Hamlet's satirical
account of this document (which he rewrites in order to send Rosencrantz and
Guildenstern to their deaths):

With, ho, such bugs and goblins in my life,
That on the supervise, no leisure bated,
No, not to stay the grinding of the ax,
My head should be struck off. (5.2.22–25)

But even though the English enterprise fails and Hamlet escapes, the King
has already developed, with Laertes, a "device,/ Under the which he shall not
choose but fall" (4.7.64–65). It will be the perfect triple plot:

And for his death no wind of blame shall breathe,
But even his mother shall uncharge the practice
And call it accident. (66–68).

Here is that characteristic word "practice" for the villain's ingenious plotting.
The word is repeated shortly afterword in the King's "pass of practice" (138).

Finally, in the fencing scene between Hamlet and Laertes in Act V, scene ii, the
Queen carouses to Hamlet's fortune (290) from the chalice into which Claudius
has thrown the poisoned "union" (273), or pearl. Hamlet cannot be persuaded
to drink, but Gertrude insists. Claudius warns her very curtly: "Gertrude, do not
drink" (291). This warning, however, does not dissuade her. Knowing that the
drink is poisoned, the King says only, in an aside: "It is the poisoned cup; it is
too late" (293). He makes no attempt at all to stop her and to save her life. A few
lines further the Queen knows exactly what has happened:

No, no, the drink, the drink! O my dear Hamlet!
The drink, the drink! I am poisoned. (310–11)

We remember that in the King's attempt to persuade Laertes to join the
conspiracy, he spoke of his great devotion to his wife:

She is so conjunctive to my life and soul,
That, as the star moves not but in his sphere,
I could not but by her. (4.7.14–16)

"Conjunctive" means closely linked or in conjunction, like stars or planets. But if Claudius is so closely tied to Gertrude, why does he let her die so casually by drinking from the poisoned cup? I think there is no way of answering this, except to note how hard and cynical the King is. Throughout the play he is represented, at least by Hamlet, as lustful and intemperate and rushing into an adulterate and incestuous marriage. But the villainous Claudius triumphs over the passionate Claudius, and he lets his wife be poisoned right before his eyes. The King is thus responsible for three murders: (1) of his brother, old Hamlet, by pouring poison in his ear; (2) of his wife, Queen Gertrude, by remaining silent while she drinks from the poisoned chalice; and (3) of his stepson Hamlet, whom he sends to be murdered in England, but, when he escapes, to kill him relentlessly in his ingenious triple plot. The King must also be held accountable for the deaths of Rosencrantz and Guildenstern and of Laertes, whom he draws so unscrupulously into the revenge plot against Hamlet. As Laertes says just before his death: "The King, the King's to blame" (5.2.321).

There is a whole set of words and images related to secrecy that develop the role of Claudius as villain. In the Ghost's report of his murder, his brother surprised him while he was taking his postprandial nap in his orchard:

Upon my secure hour thy uncle stole
With juice of cursed hebona in a vial,
And in the porches of my ears did pour
The leperous distillment. . . . (1.5.61–64)

"Secure" is used in its Latinate sense of without care or anxiety. The King is enjoying a peaceful sleep. Note that Claudius is a poisoner who does not confront his victim directly, but pours the "juice of cursed hebona" in his ears and murders surreptitiously. That is why in the *Mousetrap* play, where Hamlet will test the Ghost's narrative, he asks Horatio to carefully observe his uncle: "If his occulted guilt/ Do not itself unkennel" (3.2.82–83). Again, "occulted" (the only use in Shakespeare) is something hidden, and "unkennel" is an animal word used for driving a fox out of the hole in which it has been hiding.

At the end of the play, in Horatio's summary of the action, there is strong emphasis on the role of secrecy and chance, in what is effectively a summary of the plot. Horatio will speak

Of carnal, bloody, and unnatural acts,
Of accidental judgments, casual [by chance] slaughters,
Of deaths put on by cunning and forced cause,
And, in this upshot, purposes mistook
Fall'n on the inventors' heads. (5.2.382–86)

"Cunning and forced cause" are Claudius's *modus operandi*. His actions are all contrived and plotted, although made to appear as if they happen by chance. That is why his triple plot against Hamlet in the final scene (with the cooptation of Laertes) comes to naught. In its excess and in its striving for spontaneity, it undoes itself.

Claudius works through his spies, Rosencrantz and Guildenstern, who are summoned to find out what is troubling Hamlet. Their role in Shakespeare's play is brilliantly reimagined in Tom Stoppard's play, *Rosencrantz and Guildenstern Are Dead* (1967). It is typical of Claudius, and of Polonius too, to work through spies and eavesdropping—what the King calls "lawful espials" (3.1.32)—as if secrecy will produce much more valuable information than can be obtained by open investigation. We first meet Rosencrantz and Guildenstern at the beginning of Act II, scene ii. The King makes it clear that "The need we have to use you did provoke/ Our hasty sending" (3–4). They are to investigate Hamlet's "transformation" (5), and Claudius's words define their role:

> to gather
> So much as from occasion you may glean,
> Whether aught to us unknown afflicts him thus,
> That opened lies within our remedy. (15–18)

Their restricted role is like that of Cornelius and Voltemand, whom the King dispatches to Norway (I, ii), or like that of Reynaldo, whom Polonius sends to spy on his son in Paris (II, i). So Rosencrantz and Guildenstern follow right after the scene with Reynaldo, which helps to define their function.

The Queen indicates that the spies will be well rewarded: "Your visitation shall receive such thanks/ As fits a king's remembrance" (2.2.25–26). Rosencrantz and Guildenstern are humble and serviceable villains. They are even comic, as in the exchange between the King and Queen:

> *King.* Thanks, Rosencrantz and gentle Guildenstern.
> *Queen.* Thanks, Guildenstern and gentle Rosencrantz. (33–34)

They are treated like interchangeable twins without any individual identity. Guildenstern's parting remark is already insidious: "Heavens make our presence and our practices/ Pleasant to him!" (38–39). There is again that villain's word "practices" that is used later by the King in his plot to kill Hamlet with "A sword unbated, and, in a pass of practice,/ Requite him for your father" (4.7.138–39), and also by Laertes, who says about his unbated and envenomed sword by which he has been killed: "The foul practice/ Hath turned itself on me" (5.2.318–19).

By the time Rosencrantz and Guildenstern meet with Hamlet toward the middle of this long scene, they have become much more confident and self-assured. As old school friends, Hamlet is glad to see them, but they are soon attempting to glean information about his state of mind, specifically his "ambition" (256, 261, 262, 265). They are not to be put off, but their old friend Hamlet is growing suspicious: "Were you not sent for? Is it your own inclining? Is it a free visitation?" (280–81). Guildenstern must finally admit: "My lord, we were sent for" (300).

After the *Mousetrap* play, the two become increasingly insidious. Guildenstern is the messenger from the Queen, who wants to see Hamlet in her closet, or private room. Rosencrantz reports on the Queen's mood: "your behavior hath struck her into amazement and admiration [wonder]" (3.2.333–34). But Hamlet is wary of his old friends and forces them to admit that just as they cannot play on the recorders that are brought on stage, so too they cannot play on him:

You would play upon me; you would seem to know my stops; you would
pluck out the heart of my mystery. . . . 'Sblood, do you think I am easier to be
played on than a pipe? Call me what instrument you will, though you can fret
[vex] me, you cannot play upon me. (372–74, 378–80)

In the next scene (III, iii), the King sends them to England as guards for Hamlet, with the sealed commission ordering Hamlet's death. In this scene, too, Rosencrantz and Guildenstern speak a lot of empty rhetoric about the grandness and dangers of being King. For example, Guildenstern says:

Most holy and religious fear it is
To keep those many many bodies safe
That live and feed upon your Majesty. (8–10)

Of course, they don't know the nefarious purpose of their voyage. The King, who has written the order to kill Hamlet, speaks only in evasive terms: "For we will fetters put about this fear,/ Which now goes too free-footed" (25–26). The voyage to England promises to cure the "hectic" that rages in Claudius's blood (4.3.66).

When Hamlet escapes and is brought back to Denmark by the pirates, he reports his adventures to Horatio, who surmises that Rosencrantz and Guildenstern are still headed to instant death in England—they "go to't" (5.2.56). Hamlet is unsympathetic because they have brought their fate on themselves:

Why, man, they did make love to this employment.
They are not near my conscience; their defeat

Does by their own insinuation grow.
'Tis dangerous when the baser nature comes
Between the pass and fell incensèd points
Of mighty opposites. (57–62)

Like Polonius, whom Hamlet stabs in Act III, scene iv, Rosencrantz and
Guildenstern are meddlers and mere agents of the King. They deserve what
they get.

It is ironic that, at the end of the play, the King's ambassador to England
should proudly announce

That Rosencrantz and Guildenstern are dead.
Where should we have our thanks? (5.2.372–73)

Not from Claudius, but it is at this point that Tom Stoppard conceives his play.

Polonius, the King's chief counselor, is definitely not a villain in the sense
that he doesn't intend to kill anyone so far as we can tell, but he seems to
be the mastermind behind Claudius's ascension to the throne. Nothing in the
play accuses him of being complicit in the murder of Hamlet's father. He is
definitely not a comic character either, although he has many of the failings
of old age. He should not be played as a bumbling buffoon either, despite the
fact that he is often seen that way in many modern productions—it is a facile
interpretation of the character. Whatever his failings, he is a crafty politician,
very important to Claudius, who is constantly consulting him. We understand
him best in Act II, scene i, when he is sending Reynaldo to spy on his son in
Paris. Reynaldo plays much the same role as Rosencrantz and Guildenstern.
Polonius gives him specific directions on how to proceed. He is to put on
Laertes "What forgeries you please; marry none so rank/ As may dishonor
him" (20–21) in order to feel out what his friends and companions may say
in reply. Polonius is aware of the need to be discreet:

But breathe his faults so quaintly
That they may seem the taints of liberty,
The flash and outbreak of a fiery mind,
A savageness in unreclaimèd blood,
Of general assault. (31–35)

This is what Polonius calls "a fetch of warrant" (38), meaning a stratagem
that is technically warranted or justified.

This scene gives us a good insight into Polonius's politic methods, which
he is very proud of. He lectures Reynaldo on how an older and wiser man
should proceed:

See you now—
Your bait of falsehood take this carp of truth,
And thus do we of wisdom and of reach [far-reaching capacity],
With windlasses [devious courses] and with assays of bias,
By indirections find directions out. (62–66)

"Assays of bias" is a bowling term. The course is curved, or on the bias, so that the bowler does not aim directly at the jack, or target ball.

When Polonius comes to the King and Queen in the next scene (II,ii), he is bursting with pride (and verbiage) to report on Hamlet's love-madness:

And I do think, or else this brain of mine
Hunts not the trail of policy so sure
As it hath used to do, that I have found
The very cause of Hamlet's lunacy. (46–49)

"Policy" is a key term for villains because it indicates actions that are devious or crooked, if not actually criminal. A Machiavellian was thought to be an expert in policy, a politician who believed that the end justifies the means. When Hamlet is queried about what he has done with Polonius's body in Act IV, scene iii, he replies that "A certain convocation of politic worms are e'en at him" (19–21). He is mocking Polonius's boasted skill in statecraft, as he is also in the graveyard scene (V,i), where he comments on the gravedigger throwing up skulls:

This might be the pate of a politician, which this ass now o'erreaches, one
that would circumvent God, might it not? (79–81)

This is not specifically about Polonius, but a "politician" and one who practices policy all have strongly negative connotations.

"Policy" is used frequently in Shakespeare to mean cunning and deceit, as in Hotspur's defense of Mortimer: "Never did bare and rotten policy/ Color her working with such deadly wounds" (*1 Henry IV* 1.3.107–8), or by Thersites in *Troilus and Cressida*:

O'the t'other side, the policy of those crafty swearing rascals—that
stale old mouse-eaten dry cheese, Nestor, and that same dog-fox
Ulysses—is not proved worth a blackberry. (5.4.9–12)

It is interesting that, right before Hamlet meets with the Ghost, we have a quiet domestic scene with Polonius and his son and daughter (I,iii). Here we see Polonius at home, but he practices the same crafty and politic methods that he does in the court of Denmark. With great circumlocution and ceremony, he gives Laertes, who is leaving for Paris, a "few precepts" (58) that turn out to be much more than a few and are a collection of proverbial clichés about manners and morals, including the oft quoted "to thine own self be true" (78).

When he turns his attention to his daughter, he seems much more direct than when he advises Reynaldo in Act II, scene i. He wants to know about Ophelia's relations with Hamlet. Polonius plays the heavy father in this scene, like Capulet when his daughter Juliet refuses to marry Paris (*Romeo and Juliet* III,v). Ophelia seems to be overwhelmed by her imperious father. She speaks little but confesses everything he wants to know about Hamlet: "He hath, my lord, of late made many tenders/ Of his affection to me" (99–100). Notice that she addresses her father as my lord.

In his impatience, Polonius waxes both satirical and colloquial:

Affection pooh! You speak like a green girl
Unsifted in such perilous circumstance.
Do you believe his tenders, as you call them? (101–3)

Ophelia is crushed and says only "I do not know, my lord, what I should think" (104). Her father then takes charge of his daughter's subjectivity:

Marry, I will teach you. Think yourself a baby
That you have ta'en these tenders for true pay. (105–6)

Polonius puns mercilessly on "tenders." At the end of the scene he commands his daughter to break off all relations with Hamlet. There is a speech-like intimacy in his final line: "Look to't, I charge you. Come your ways" (135). Ophelia can only answer: "I shall obey, my lord" (136).

In Act III, scene i, Ophelia functions like a property that her father places on stage, with a book of devotions, to confront Hamlet, so that he and the King can "bestow ourselves" (44) as eavesdroppers. It is pitiful how passive and drained of energy Ophelia has become. At the end of this scene she can only bewail her fate: "O, woe is me/ T' have seen what I have seen, see what I see!" (163–64). Polonius dismisses his daughter as an insignificant presence:

How now, Ophelia?
You need not tell us what Lord Hamlet said;
We heard it all. (181–83)

The test of whether Hamlet is mad for love is strictly a matter between Polonius and the King.

Polonius is also eavesdropping in the Queen's closet in Act III, scene iv. When he speaks in order to help the Queen, who thinks that her son is about to murder her, Hamlet immediately thrusts his rapier through the arras and kills him. He does it with a swaggering gambler's oath: "How now? A rat? Dead for a ducat, dead!" (25). Hamlet probably thinks that he has killed the King, but he treats Polonius much as he does Rosencrantz and Guildenstern: "They are not near my conscience" (5.2.58). Hamlet thinks of Polonius as directly allied with the King and therefore his mortal enemy. His elegy for him is sarcastic:

Indeed, this counselor
Is now most still, most secret, and most grave,
Who was in life a foolish prating knave. (3.4.214–16)

To Hamlet, Polonius is always a knave, albeit foolish and prating.

It is ironic that Polonius seems to predict his own death when he tells *Hamlet* that he once "did enact Julius Caesar. I was killed i' th' Capitol; Brutus killed me" (3.2.105–6). Hamlet has only a punning reply: "It was a brute part of him to kill so capital a calf there" (107–8). It is interesting that Polonius should imagine himself as the mighty Julius Caesar, if only in a play. In *Hamlet*, however, he always remains Claudius's factotum.

Laertes, too, is the King's agent. When he returns from France, he speaks in the overblown rhetoric of the stage revenger. He and his followers break into the King's throne room and seem about to usurp control of the kingdom. But the King is confident that he can put down this impetuous and foolish young man. He speaks mockingly of Laertes's rebellion as "giantlike" (4.5.121) and tells the Queen that he doesn't need her protection:

Let him go, Gertrude. Do not fear our person.
There's such divinity doth hedge a king
That treason can but peep to what it would,
Acts little of his will. (122–25)

So Claudius mollifies the enraged Laertes, who rants like a villain:

To hell allegiance, vows to the blackest devil,
Conscience and grace to the profoundest pit!
I dare damnation. (131–33)

The King skillfully manages to calm his empty ardor.

In Act IV, scene vii, when the King, trying to measure Laertes's commitment to revenge, asks him:

what would you undertake
To show yourself in deed your father's son
More than in words? (124–26)

Laertes has provided sufficient words, but now he shocks the King with his blunt reply: "To cut his throat i' th' church!" (126). The King is taken aback and utters expected moral platitudes: "No place indeed should murder sanctuarize;/ Revenge should have no bounds" (127–28). But he continues with the wise idea to keep Laertes out of sight: "But, good Laertes,/ Will you do this? Keep close within your chamber" (128–29). A chamber is where one sleeps, a perfect containment for such a loose cannon as Laertes.

He is also a poisoner, like the King himself, and he participates with enthusiasm in the King's triple plot to kill Hamlet. He informs Claudius that he will not only use a rapier that is unbated, or unprotected on its tip, but he will also anoint it with poison:

I bought an unction of a mountebank,
So mortal that, but dip a knife in it,
Where it draws blood, no cataplasm [poultice] so rare,
Collected from all simples [medicinal herbs] that have virtue
Under the moon, can save the thing from death
That is but scratched withal. I'll touch my point
With this contagion, that, if I gall him slightly,
It may be death. (141–48)

Laertes is eager to participate in Claudius's plot, and he even inspires the King to think of something else: "Soft, let me see./ We'll make a solemn wager on your cunnings—/I ha't!" (154–56). We see the King, like Iago, improvising his plot, and he now hits upon the idea of poisoning the chalice of wine with a union, or pearl. The project of killing Hamlet stimulates the inventiveness of both Laertes and Claudius.

In the fencing scene in Act V, scene ii, Shakespeare is eager to show the reconciliation of Hamlet and Laertes, almost too eager, because it seems rather rushed and undeveloped. Laertes asserts that he will hit Hamlet now with his rapier, the King doesn't think so, and then Laertes says in a remarkable aside: "And yet it is almost against my conscience" (297). This is, structurally, like the King's aside in Act III, scene i (49–54). It reveals something important about Laertes's inner being. When they exchange rapiers and Laertes is struck with the unbated and poisoned sword, he confesses to Osric: "I am justly killed with mine own treachery" (308).

After the Queen drinks from the poisoned chalice and dies, Laertes falls. He confesses to Hamlet that he is slain and that

The foul practice
Hath turned itself on me. Lo, here I lie,
Never to rise again. (318–20)

Before asking forgiveness from Hamlet, the dying Laertes clearly places the blame on the play's villain: "The King, the King's to blame" (321). He is importunate to recover Hamlet's good will:

Exchange forgiveness with me, noble Hamlet.
Mine and my father's death come not upon thee,
Nor thine on me! (330–32)

He seems to be forgetting that Hamlet stabbed his father Polonius in Act III, scene iv, but in the end his thirst for revenge is quenched

Claudius is a secret villain who is not sardonic or sportive like Aaron, Richard Duke of Gloucester, Iago, and Shylock. He works through intermediaries, like his spies Rosencrantz and Guildenstern and his chief counselor Polonius. He even manages to divert to his purposes the mutinous Laertes, who seems about to usurp the kingdom of Denmark. Claudius is not a particularly inventive speaker like Shakespeare's previous villains, but he seems a commanding and effective King. When he dispatches Cornelius and Voltemand to deal with Fortinbras, we are impressed by his curt sense of purpose: "So much for him" (1.2.25). Despite his sympathetic soliloquy in Act III, scene iii, the King knows that he cannot pray—that his prayers are useless without true penitence. Claudius is a killer like Richard, Duke of Gloucester: he is responsible for the deaths of his brother (old Hamlet), Hamlet, Laertes, Gertrude, Rosencrantz and Guildenstern, and Polonius, too, if we remember that he was spying for the King behind the arras in Gertrude's "closet." The fact that King Claudius is conscious of his guilt obviously doesn't prevent him from murdering freely. The "hectic" that rages in his blood (4.3.66) must be appeased.

NOTE

1. A. C. Bradley seriously undervalues the role of Claudius as Hamlet's antagonist in this play. For example, he says: "In *Hamlet,* though we have a villain, he is a small one" (p.82), and also on p. 169: Claudius "had a small nature. . . . He had the inclination of natures physically weak and morally small towards intrigue and crooked dealing. His instinctive predilection was for poison. . . ." A. C. Bradley, *Shakespearean Tragedy*, London, 1950. First published, 1904. See also Maurice Charney, *Style in "Hamlet,"* Princeton, NJ: Princeton University Press, 1969, especially Ch. 9 on Claudius and Ch. 10 on Polonius, and *Hamlet's Fictions*, New York, NY: Routledge, 1988.

Chapter 6

Macbeth

Macbeth as villain has some superficial resemblances to Richard, Duke of Gloucester, in his ruthless pursuit of the crown, but Macbeth has none of the jocularity and histrionic quality that Richard inherits from the Vice figure of the morality plays. Macbeth is Shakespeare's most developed experiment in the protagonist as villain-hero.[1] Shylock and Claudius are sympathetic in individual speeches and soliloquies, but Macbeth seems to be sympathetic throughout the play because he is so acutely aware of the horror of his crimes. His conscience always bothers him, even at the very end of the play when he is fallen into a deep despair.[2]

He begins the play as a military hero, who has conquered the "merciless Macdonwald" (1.2.9) and "unseamed him from the nave [navel] to th' chops [jaws]" (22). The "bleeding Captain" reports on the battle to the King, who is impressed with the heroic exploits of Macbeth and Banquo. They appear in the second scene with the Witches (I,iii). In the context of the first and third scenes, with thunder and lightning and foul weather, we know that something portentous is about to happen. Macbeth's first line is: "So foul and fair a day I have not seen" (1.3.38), and we are plunged into moral ambiguity. His next line is to question the Witches: "Speak, if you can: what are you?" (47). The questions continue in his next speech. He is aware that the Witches are "imperfect speakers" (70) who convey "strange intelligence" (76). They are not yet the "juggling fiends..../That palter with us in a double sense" (5.8.19–20) that they become at the end of the play. Of course, they answer none of Macbeth's questions and vanish suddenly at line 78.

Banquo is more skeptical about the Witches than Macbeth: "The earth hath bubbles as the water has,/And these are of them" (79–80). He even thinks they may be an illusion:

Or have we eaten on the insane root
That takes the reason prisoner? (84–85)

But when Ross, on a mission from the King, calls Macbeth Thane of
Cawdor, Macbeth is astounded: "The Thane of Cawdor lives: why do you
dress me/In borrowed robes?" (108–9). Thus begins the teasing ambiguity
of the Witches.

Macbeth is suitably impressed, and he says to Banquo:

Do you not hope your children shall be kings,
When those that gave the Thane of Cawdor to me
Promised no less to them? (118–20)

Banquo, however, is wary:

And oftentimes, to win us to our harm,
The instruments of darkness tell us truths,
Win us with honest trifles, to betray 's
In deepest consequence. (123–26)

But Macbeth cannot be shaken out of his optimism; as he says, aside, to
Banquo:

Two truths are told,
As happy prologues to the swelling act
Of the imperial theme. (127–29)

Notice that he is already speaking of "the imperial theme," as if this were
the necessary third step in what the Witches have promised. Macbeth is sufficiently aware that what the Witches speak is riddling: "This supernatural
soliciting/Cannot be ill, cannot be good" (130–31). Most importantly, he
already understands that if he follows through what they prophesy, he will
have to murder the King:

If good, why do I yield to that suggestion
Whose horrid image doth unfix my hair
And make my seated heart knock at my ribs,
Against the use of nature? (134–37)

Shakespeare's villains are not generally troubled by horrid images that cause
a strong physiological reaction.

It is Macbeth's acute awareness of his mental state that separates him from
other Shakespearean villains:

> Present fears
> Are less than horrible imaginings.
> My thought, whose murder yet is but fantastical [imaginary],
> Shakes so my single state of man that function
> Is smothered in surmise, and nothing is
> But what is not. (137–42)

Again, we have that key word "horrible," which matches "horrid" in line 135. Macbeth already imagines himself as a murderer and foresees the effects, both physiological and psychological, it will have on him.

Banquo precisely describes Macbeth's psychological condition: "Look, how our partner's rapt" (142). This is the same word he used before in addressing the Witches:

> My noble partner
> You greet with present grace and great prediction
> Of noble having and of royal hope,
> That he seems rapt withal. . . . (54–57)

"Rapt" is also Macbeth's word in his letter to his wife: he "stood rapt in the wonder" (1.5.6) at the Witches' recital. The word is not frequent in Shakespeare, but it occurs more often in this play than in any other. It is connected with "rapture," and the *Oxford English Dictionary* defines it (in its third meaning) as: "Transported with some emotion, ravished, enraptured."

So Macbeth is profoundly affected by what the Witches tell him. In an aside to Banquo, he leaves open the possibility that he may not have to do anything at all to bring on his good fortune: "If chance will have me King, why, chance may crown me,/Without my stir" (143–44). But we know from his aside in the next scene (I,iv) that he is preparing himself to murder the King:

> The Prince of Cumberland! That is a step
> On which I must fall down, or else o'erleap,
> For in my way it lies. Stars, hide your fires;
> Let not light see my black and deep desires:
> The eye wink at the hand; yet let that be
> Which the eye fears, when it is done, to see. (48–53)

Macbeth sounds like Richard, Duke of Gloucester, here, but there is no sense of the necessary murders as sport or game. I have focused on these early scenes because they make clear that Macbeth doesn't need his wife's forceful persuasions to convince him to murder the King; he is already preoccupied with this idea when he returns to Inverness castle in Act I, scene v.

Before the murder of King Duncan, Macbeth has a whole series of conscience-stricken soliloquies. He understands only too clearly the moral fault of what he is about to do and its dire consequences. His continuous awareness makes him different from other villains in Shakespeare. Act I, scene vii begins with a long soliloquy in which Macbeth ponders the moral implications of the murder he is just on the point of committing. It cannot be done quickly and successfully without thoughts of what will happen in "the life to come" (7). This is like the distinction Claudius makes in his soliloquy between what is true "In the corrupted currents of this world" as distinguished from what is true in heaven: "But 'tis not so above./There is no shuffling" (*Hamlet* 3.3.57, 60–61). So Macbeth realizes that

> We still [always] have judgment here; that we but teach
> Bloody instructions, which, being taught, return
> To plague th' inventor: this even-handed justice
> Commends th' ingredients of our poisoned chalice
> To our own lips. (1.7.8–12)

Remember that Claudius is forced to drink from his own poisoned chalice in the last scene of *Hamlet.*

Macbeth's powerful sense of his own tragedy is impressive in this soliloquy and in the many soliloquies that follow. He knows that Duncan is a guest in his castle

> in double trust:
> First, as I am his kinsman and his subject,
> Strong both against the deed; then, as his host,
> Who should against his murderer shut the door,
> Not bear the knife myself. (12–16)

This is like the violation of hospitality that Gloucester accuses Regan and Goneril of in *King Lear.* Macbeth is acutely self-judged:

> I have no spur
> To prick the sides of my intent, but only
> Vaulting ambition, which o'erleaps itself
> And falls on th' other—(25–28)

The images are from horsemanship, when the rider vaults over the saddle and comes out on the other side. But Macbeth's understanding of what is happening to him does not prevent him from murdering King Duncan; they only make it more agonizing and painful.

Macbeth's long soliloquy in Act II, scene i, "Is this a dagger which I see before me" (33), still precedes the murder of the King, which does not occur until the next scene. Macbeth seems to be speaking of an imaginary dagger, "A dagger of the mind" (38), which he sees "in form as palpable" (40) as the dagger "which now I draw" (41). This real dagger is the one with which Macbeth will kill the King:

> Thou marshal'st me the way that I was going;
> And such an instrument I was to use. (42–43)

By the feverish workings of his imagination, he already pictures the dagger, proleptically, covered with blood, as if he has already committed the murder:

> I see thee still;
> And on thy blade and dudgeon [wooden hilt] gouts of blood,
> Which was not so before. (45–47)

So the dagger is both an illusion and graphically real.

It is interesting that Macbeth personifies "withered murder" (52):

> thus with his stealthy pace,
> With Tarquin's ravishing strides, towards his design
> Moves like a ghost. (54–56)

Tarquin, in *The Rape of Lucrece*, was one of Shakespeare's first villains. Macbeth moves toward his victim like the personified Murder, and, again, he personifies the "firm-set earth" (56), asking it not to hear his steps, "which way they walk, for fear/Thy very stones prate of my whereabout" (57–58) and give him away. It is all very dream-like, with Macbeth personifying Murder and Earth, and picturing himself moving inevitably to his tragic doom.

When the deed is done in Act II, scene ii, Macbeth's main concern seems to be that he cannot answer the "God bless us" and "Amen" that Duncan's servants pronounce in their sleep. It is as if he is already experiencing the effects of the murder, which separates him from God's grace and begins the sense of despair he feels from this point on:

> But wherefore could not I pronounce "Amen"?
> I had most need of blessing, and "Amen"
> Stuck in my throat. (29–31)

This sense of having lost God's benediction makes Macbeth unique among Shakespeare's villains. Why would he expect God's "blessing" when he is in the very act of murdering the King? No doubt he has "most need of blessing" at this moment, yet it is clearly impossible.

Among Macbeth's hallucinations is the voice he hears crying

"Sleep no more!
Macbeth does murder sleep"—the innocent sleep,
Sleep that knits up the raveled sleave [silk filament] of care,
The death of each day's life, sore labor's bath,
Balm of hurt minds, great nature's second course,
Chief nourisher in life's feast—(34–39)

It is curious how much Macbeth is given to personifications in his fearful discourse—in this speech, both Sleep and Care—a characteristic of Shakespeare's earlier writing, as in *The Rape of Lucrece*.

Macbeth is preoccupied with sleep (and related words); the 32 uses are more than in any other play of Shakespeare. Insomnia is uniquely the effect of murder and tragedy in this play. The protagonist cannot let go of the frightening anticipation of sleeplessness that accompanies guilt:

Still it cried "Sleep no more!" to all the house:
"Glamis hath murdered sleep, and therefore Cawdor
Shall sleep no more: Macbeth shall sleep no more." (40–42)

Macbeth's fears echo those of the guilt-ridden King Henry IV, whose long apostrophe to sleep ends with a careworn conclusion: "Uneasy lies the head that wears a crown" (*2 Henry IV* 3.1.31).

After the murder of King Duncan, Macbeth continues on to other murders that are necessitated by the first murder: "To be thus is nothing, but [except] to be safely thus" (3.1.48). Banquo (and his son Fleance) are next because of what the Witches have promised Banquo, that he will be "father to a line of kings" (60). In a long soliloquy, Macbeth tries to engage with the Witches' promises to Banquo:

There is none but he
Whose being I do fear: and under him
My genius is rebuked, as it is said
Mark Antony's was by Caesar. (54–57)

This looks forward to events in *Antony and Cleopatra*. Macbeth, with the murderers he has hired, sounds a lot like Richard, Duke of Gloucester here. We note a steady deterioration in his sensitivity until he reaches the utter despair of Act V, scene v.

But he is already well on the way in the next scene (III,ii), as he tells his wife of his profound uneasiness and sense of futility:

> We have scorched [slashed] the snake, not killed it:
> She'll close [heal] and be herself, whilst our poor malice
> Remains in danger of her former tooth. (13–15)

Notice that he now speaks of the murder of King Duncan as "our poor malice," a seemingly trivial and ill-intentioned affair. Macbeth describes vividly his and his wife's physical and spiritual state:

> these terrible dreams
> That shake us nightly: better be with the dead,
> Whom we, to gain our peace, have sent to peace,
> Than on the torture of the mind to lie
> In restless ecstasy. (18–22)

"Ecstasy" is Shakespeare's usual word for madness or mental and emotional frenzy.

But Banquo and Fleance are "assailable" (39), and Macbeth seeks to undo the fateful pronouncements of the Witches (the Weïrd Sisters, who function like the Fates). At the end of the scene, he conceals from his wife his intention to kill Banquo and Fleance: "Be innocent of the knowledge, dearest chuck,/ Till thou applaud the deed" (45–46). "Chuck," or chick, is a familiar term of endearment, but it is interesting that Macbeth doesn't confide in his wife at this point. The murders that he plans have a new urgency that seems to involve all of nature:

> Come, seeling [that closes the eyes] night,
> Scarf up the tender eye of pitiful day,
> And with thy bloody and invisible hand
> Cancel and tear to pieces that great bond
> Which keeps me pale! (46–50)

"That great bond" is a legal term that defines Macbeth's essential humanity. The scene ends with an apocalyptic metaphor:

> Light thickens, and the crow
> Makes wing to th' rooky wood.
> Good things of day begin to droop and drowse,
> Whiles night's black agents to their preys do rouse. (50–53)

The crow (also called the rook) is a bird that feeds on carrion.

It is curious how many birds of prey are mentioned in this play; they serve as "night's black agents." (We are reminded of Hitchcock's baleful movie *The Birds* of 1963). In addition to the crow and the rook, we have also the raven, which is "hoarse/ That croaks the fatal entrance of Duncan" (1.5.39–40). In Act II, scene ii, there is "the owl that shrieked, the fatal bellman/ Which gives the stern'st good-night" (3–4) and afterwards screams (15). In Act II, scene iii, the owl is "the obscure bird," which, as a portent, "Clamored the livelong night" (61–62). Also among the portents is:

> A falcon, tow'ring in her pride of place,
> Was by a mousing owl hawked at and killed. (2.4.12–13)

These strange events signal perturbations in nature, since an owl's ordinary diet is mice. We also have kites (3.4.74, carnivorous birds in the raven family), vultures (4.3.74), and loons (5.3.11). In addition, there are Hecate's ministers, the bat who wings "His cloistered flight" (3.2.41) and "The shard-borne beetle with his drowsy hums" (42), which rings "night's yawning peal" (43). All these flying things associated with black night are rapacious and portend something diabolical, like the murders with which they are linked.

When the Ghost of the murdered Banquo appears at Macbeth's feast and sits in his place, Macbeth takes this as an evil portent, according to the proverbial "Murder will out" (Tilley M1315):

> It will have blood, they say: blood will have blood.
> Stones have been known to move and trees to speak;
> Augures [auguries] and understood relations have
> By maggot-pies [magpies] and choughs [a bird in the crow family] and rooks
> brought forth
> The secretist man of blood. (3.4.123–27)

Notice how powerful the birds are—and augury is a form of divination by the flight of birds—as signifiers of secret murder. All of nature is conspiring to avenge the deaths of Banquo and King Duncan, and to reveal even the most concealed man of blood.

We now move to Macduff, who has absented himself from Macbeth's great feast. His murder is the next in a seemingly endless succession that Macbeth must accomplish in order to secure his initial murder—and to be able to sleep again. Once more, he doesn't confide in his wife, but speaks with a new weariness of spirit:

> I am in blood
> Stepped in so far that, should I wade no more,
> Returning were as tedious as go o'er. (3.4.137–39)

This is a frightening image of the river of blood, a nightmarish image, with the curious word "tedious" to mark Macbeth's growing apathy.

It is like Richard III's image for his constrained and endless commitment to murder. He sees that he must now be married to his brother Edward's daughter, Elizabeth, but he proceeds with a singular lack of enthusiasm:

> Murder her brothers and then marry her!
> Uncertain way of gain! But I am in
> So far in blood that sin will pluck on sin.
> Tear-falling pity dwells not in this eye. (*Richard III* 4.2.61–64)

It is as if Richard, like Macbeth, is caught up in a cycle of continuous murder that proceeds outside of his conscious will. This is a proverbial idea: "Crimes (Mischiefs) are made secure by greater crimes (mischiefs)" (Tilley C826). The sentiment probably originates in Seneca's *Agamemnon*.[3]

Macduff is absent from his castle, but the murder of his wife and children in Act IV, scene ii, is a spectacle of unimaginable cruelty, like the blinding of Gloucester in *King Lear* (III, vii). It is performed by nameless murderers, like the killing of Banquo, and not by Macbeth himself (who kills King Duncan). Macduff underscores the savagery; it is because Macbeth

> has no children. All my pretty ones?
> Did you say all? O hell-kite! All?
> What, all my pretty chickens and their dam
> At one fell swoop? (4.3.216–19)

Macduff cannot believe what he hears, and there is a certain nostalgia in his grief: "I cannot but remember such things were,/That were most precious to me" (222–23). Notice, too, the bird of prey image for Macbeth the murderer: "O hell-kite."

By Act V, Macbeth is falling into despair, indicted by his remarkable insight into his spiritual condition:

> I have lived long enough. My way of life
> Is fall'n into the sear [withered], the yellow leaf,
> And that which should accompany old age,
> As honor, love, obedience, troops of friends,
> I must not look to have; but, in their stead,
> Curses not loud but deep, mouth-honor, breath,
> Which the poor heart would fain deny, and dare not. (5.3.22–28)

This echoes the imagery of Sonnet 73, "That time of year thou may'st in me behold." Macbeth's sensitivity of the earlier scenes centering on the murder of King Duncan has disappeared. He is now apathetic and isolated, without

friends, and feeling only the hollowness of the purely ceremonial "mouth-
honor."

He is acutely aware of his desiccation of spirit. When he hears the *"cry
within of women"* (5.5.7 s.d.), announcing the death of his wife, Macbeth
comments on his own apathy, very different from his earlier fears and
imaginings:

> I have almost forgot the taste of fears:
> The time has been, my senses would have cooled
> To hear a night-shriek, and my fell of hair
> Would at a dismal treatise rouse and stir
> As life were in 't. I have supped full with horrors.
> Direness, familiar to my slaughterous thoughts,
> Cannot once start [startle] me. (9–15)

We are made to feel that Macbeth's sensibility has been dulled during the
course of the play, that a great deal of time has passed, and that he is now an
old man waiting to die.

That is why he seems to be wearily indifferent to his wife's death:

> She should have died hereafter;
> There would have been a time for such a word. (17–18)

Presumably, this is not a proper time for Lady Macbeth to die, now that her
unfeeling husband cannot properly mourn her—perhaps it will be better
"hereafter." Or it could mean that she has died at an unpropitious time for
Macbeth and for the state. Macbeth's ambiguous words should be interpreted
in terms of the despairing speech that follows:

> Tomorrow, and tomorrow, and tomorrow
> Creeps in this petty pace from day to day,
> To the last syllable of recorded time;
> And all our yesterdays have lighted fools
> The way to dusty death. (19–23)

This is a speech about the endlessness and meaningless of time. The last syl-
lable of recorded time does not lead to the Day of Judgment, as we would
expect, but only to an empty void. It is the lack of any significance that is the
marker of Macbeth's deep depression. He despairs in the theological sense
of a lack of belief in the possibility of God's grace and beneficence. Like a

number of Shakespeare's villains, he is at this point technically an atheist, and now ready for death.

That is the presumed meaning of the end of the speech:

> Out, out, brief candle!
> Life's but a walking shadow, a poor player
> That struts and frets his hour upon the stage
> And then is heard no more. It is a tale
> Told by an idiot, full of sound and fury
> Signifying nothing. (23–28)

It is interesting that Shakespeare should choose to express Macbeth's despair in acting imagery, which offers an excellent way of distinguishing between appearance and reality. The "poor" player is not necessarily a bad actor, but someone who illustrates the shortness and noisy fury of a life without significance. Macbeth, the conscience-stricken murderer, is commenting on his own life. The murders he has committed were all for naught because his ambition did not bring him either content or security, represented by the inability to sleep. His life has been full of perturbation, ending now in complete emptiness.

Lady Macbeth is not a villain in her own right,[4] but we need to think of her as the enabling factor in the murder of the King. It is clear that Macbeth is seriously contemplating this murder well before Act I, scene v, where we see his wife reading his letter about his encounter with the Witches. What is remarkable about Lady Macbeth's long soliloquy in this scene is her uncanny insight into the mind of her husband. She fears that his compassionate temperament will prevent him from committing murder. His nature

> is too full o' th' milk of human kindness
> To catch the nearest way. Thou wouldst be great,
> Art not without ambition, but without
> The illness [evil] should attend it. What thou wouldst highly,
> That wouldst thou holily; wouldst not play false,
> And yet wouldst wrongly win. Thou'dst have, great Glamis,
> That which cries "Thus thou must do" if thou have it;
> And that which rather thou dost fear to do
> Than wishest should be undone. (18–26)

Presumably, Lady Macbeth has none of these sentimental reservations, so that it is important that she "pour" her "spirits" into her husband's ear (27). She doesn't need to convince him of the necessity for the murder, but only to spur him on.

In another soliloquy before Macbeth arrives—and it is significant how important soliloquies are in this play for both protagonists—she already considers the entrance of Duncan into her castle as "fatal" (1.5.40). She calls upon spirits, presumably diabolic spirits, "That tend on mortal [murderous] thoughts" (42), to effect radical gender changes:

> unsex me here,
> And fill me, from the crown to the toe, top-full
> Of direst cruelty! Make thick my blood,
> Stop up th' access and passage to remorse [compassion],
> That no compunctious visitings of nature
> Shake my fell [deadly] purpose, nor keep peace between
> Th' effect and it! (42–48)

I take "unsex" to mean that the spirits she invokes should remove all kind and milky feminine traits and make her a female warrior or Amazon, like Volumnia in *Coriolanus*. She prays that her blood, which carries human emotions, be made "thick" and unfeeling.

This long passage about unsexing initiates the gender debate that is so important in the play. On one side, Macbeth needs to prove his manliness, as defined in the second scene of the play, where the "brave Macbeth" (1.2.16), the consummate warrior, unseams the "merciless Macdonwald" (9) "from the nave to th' chops" (22). It is interesting that the murderers Macbeth hires to kill Banquo and Fleance make a point of asserting their manliness (and therefore their fitness for murder). The First Murderer says: "We are men, my liege" (3.1.91). Macbeth then goes into a long discourse about various kinds of dogs, which he then applies to the Murderers:

> and so of men.
> Now if you have a station in the file,
> Not i' th' worst rank of manhood, say 't. . . . (101–3)

The distinction is most tersely put in *King Lear*, when Edmund sends a Captain to murder Lear and Cordelia in prison. The Officer boasts of his manliness:

> I cannot draw a cart, nor eat dried oats.
> If it be man's work, I'll do't. (5.3.39–40)

So the unsexing of Lady Macbeth is to make her fit to do man's work, in other words, to commit murder.

In Act I, scene vii she is completely unsympathetic to Macbeth's scruples and hesitations:

Art thou afeard
To be the same in thine own act and valor
As thou art in desire? (39–41)

Macbeth protests his valor: "I dare do all that may become a man;/ Who dares do more is none" (46–47), but these rhetorical assertions don't satisfy his wife:

What beast was 't then
That made you break this enterprise to me?
When you durst do it, then you were a man;
And to be more than what you were, you would
Be so much more the man. (47–51)

Lady Macbeth makes it clear that the only way her husband can prove his manhood is by killing the King.

She goes on, with extraordinary savagery, to reject her maternal role:

I have given suck, and know
How tender 'tis to love the babe that milks me:
I would, while it was smiling in my face,
Have plucked my nipple from his boneless gums,
And dashed the brains out, had I so sworn as you
Have done to this. (54–59)

This glorification of infanticide as a proof of her manliness shocks Macbeth—and perhaps also arouses a certain admiration:

Bring forth men-children only;
For thy undaunted mettle should compose
Nothing but males. (72–74)

Lady Macbeth's assertions of infanticide are a measure of her warrior-like valor, and they continue her earlier appeal about unsexing. She is specific about the rejection of maternal images, especially that of the nursing mother, as she invokes her diabolic spirits:

Come to my woman's breasts,
And take my milk for gall, you murd'ring ministers,
Wherever in your sightless [invisible] substances
You wait on nature's mischief! Come, thick night,
And pall thee in the dunnest smoke of hell,
That my keen knife see not the wound it makes,
Nor heaven peep through the blanket of the dark,
To cry "Hold, hold!" (48–55)

Of course, we never see Lady Macbeth's "keen knife," nor does she participate directly in the murder of King Duncan, but we understand vividly her
homicidal impulses. In a curious detail, she explains her non-participation:
"Had he not resembled/My father as he slept, I had done 't" (2.2.12–13). This
is a frightening piece of information that we remember in Lady Macbeth's
mad scene (V, i).

There is one further scene in which Lady Macbeth insistently questions
her husband's manliness, when the Ghost of Banquo appears *"and sits in
Macbeth's place"* (3.4.38 s.d.). Macbeth is appalled: "Never shake/Thy gory
locks at me" (51–52), but his wife tries to maintain the decorum of a festive
dinner. She says to him, aside, with emphatic disgust: "Are you a man?" (59).
He replies with alacrity: "Ay, and a bold one, that dare look on that/Which
might appall the devil" (60–61). But Lady Macbeth scoffs at her husband's
fears and imaginings:

> O proper stuff!
> This is the very painting of your fear.
> This is the air-drawn dagger which, you said,
> Led you to Duncan. (61–64)

In the phrase "proper stuff" we see the authentic, domestic, hen-pecking
wife, who has only contempt for her husband's supposed sensitivity:

> O, these flaws [gusts] and starts,
> Impostors to true fear, would well become
> A woman's story at a winter's fire,
> Authorized [sanctioned] by her grandam. Shame itself!
> Why do you make such faces? When all's done,
> You look but on a stool. (64–69)

In the mix-up of genders, Macbeth now shows himself to be womanish compared to his wife's hearty masculinity. He is "unmanned in folly" (74), just
as earlier Lady Macbeth invoked spirits to unsex her.

Macbeth's protests are futile. When the Ghost of Banquo appears again, he
once more asserts his manliness:

> What man dare, I dare.
> Approach thou like the rugged Russian bear,
> The armed rhinoceros, or th' Hyrcan tiger;
> Take any shape but that, and my firm nerves
> Shall never tremble. (100–4)

But the Ghost will not be dictated to. It is only when it disappears that Macbeth can declare: "I am a man again" (109). None of this satisfies Lady Macbeth, and the scene ends with Macbeth's plan to murder Macduff and his household, seemingly as a way to reassert his manliness and convince his wife (although he doesn't tell her about it).

Lady Macbeth is developed very differently from her husband. She has none of his fears and sensitivities. For example, when we first hear the knocking at the gates of the castle, Macbeth is appalled by the noise, which reminds him of his bloody guilt:

> What hands are here? Ha! They pluck out mine eyes!
> Will all great Neptune's ocean wash this blood
> Clean from my hand? No; this my hand will rather
> The multitudinous seas incarnadine [redden],
> Making the green one red. (2.2.58–62)

Macbeth examines his bloody hands in a powerful stage gesture.

When Lady Macbeth enters, she immediately agrees that her "hands are of your color, but I shame/ To wear a heart so white [cowardly]" (63–64). She then makes an observation which utterly separates her from her husband: "A little water clears us of this deed;/How easy is it then!" (66–67). Macbeth thinks rather that his bloody hands will redden the infinitely large, "multitudinous seas."

All of this imagery returns in Lady Macbeth's mad scene (V, i). It is night and she enters sleep-walking *"with a taper"* (20 s.d.). The words she speaks seem to undo what she has said earlier in the play. She is preoccupied with the blood of murder, and she rubs her hands obsessively to wash them clean. She takes up lines that appeared earlier in a different context:

> Out, damned spot! Out, I say! One: two: why, then 'tis time to do 't.
> Hell is murky. Fie, my lord, fie! A soldier, and afeard? What need we fear
> who knows it, when none can call our pow'r to accompt? Yet who would have
> thought the old man to have had so much blood in him? (38–43)

Lady Macbeth's madness conveys the feeling that she has participated more directly in the murder of King Duncan than what we have seen. She has intimations of hell and damnation.

She also remembers the murder of Macduff's wife, which Macbeth hesitated even to tell her about: "The Thane of Fife had a wife. Where is she now? What, will these hands ne'er be clean?" (45–46). She speaks in sing-song rhymes like the mad Ophelia (*Hamlet* IV, v). Although she washes her hands compulsively, we know that it is all a meaningless ritual. The gesture is a powerful reenactment of her guilt: "Here's the smell of the blood still. All the perfumes of Arabia will not sweeten this little hand. Oh, oh, oh!" (53–55). These lines seem to be remembered in *King Lear* when the blind Gloucester says to Lear: "O, let me kiss that hand!" and the mad King says only: "Let me wipe it first, it smells of mortality" (4.6.128–29). Again, there is a specific answer here to Macbeth that extends the scene of Banquo's Ghost (III, iv): "Wash your hands; put on your nightgown; look not so pale! I tell you again, Banquo's buried. He cannot come out on 's grave" (65–67).

Finally, Lady Macbeth's speech picks up bits and pieces from the whole play: "To bed, to bed! There's knocking at the gate. Come, come, come, come, give me your hand! What's done cannot be undone. To bed, to bed, to bed!" (69–72). The repetition of "to bed" reminds us of how closely sleeplessness is linked with Lady Macbeth's sense of overpowering guilt—and Macbeth's too—which is only now beginning to manifest itself. Lady Macbeth is not a villain, but she has murderous and savage thoughts that are like her husband's. She helps to define Macbeth's role as a villain-hero, although, until her mad scene, she has none of his compunctions about killing. The soliloquy in her mad scene would be more appropriate to Macbeth if he were not so drowned in despair and spiritual aridity.

Macbeth has a special status in Shakespeare as a villain-hero. In other words, even while he is engaged in the murders of Duncan, Banquo, and Macduff's wife and children, he feels tremendous guilt and agonizes with himself over his ill-doing. We feel sympathetic to Macbeth in his soul-searching and in his spiritual crisis, as we do to Claudius when he examines his conscience in his long soliloquy in *Hamlet* (III, iii). Macbeth's (and Lady Macbeth's too) guilty conscience is expressed by the inability to sleep. Macbeth is also troubled by the imagery of birds of prey. The play raises significant gender issues, especially in what it means to be a man. Lady Macbeth unsexes herself to become a female warrior, and she accuses her husband of a lack of manliness in the encounter with Banquo's ghost. Lady Macbeth's role in the play serves to develop our understanding of her husband. She doesn't persuade him to murder Duncan, but she has acute understanding of his thinking, that he "wouldst not play false,/And yet wouldst wrongly win" (1.5.22–23). At the end of the play, she moves sharply away from her facile comment, "A little water clears us of this deed" (2.2.66) to the passionate guilt of her mad speeches, whereas her extremely sensitive husband moves in the opposite direction to despair and spiritual desiccation.

NOTES

1. See the original observations of E. A. J. Honigmann on "*Macbeth*: The Murderer as Victim," which is Chapter 8 of *Shakespeare: Seven Tragedies: The Dramatist's Manipulation of Response*, 2 ed., London, 2002. Honigmann also speaks insightfully about Iago in Chapter 6: "Secret Motives in *Othello*."

2. See Kenneth Muir, "Image and Symbol in 'Macbeth,'" *Shakespeare Survey*, 19 (1966), 45–54.

3. See the note in the Arden edition of *King Richard III*, ed. Antony Hammond, London, 1981, p. 268.

4. Bradley makes a point of the "literalism" (p. 372) of Lady Macbeth's mind: "But the limitations of her mind appear most in the point where she is most strongly contrasted with Macbeth,—in her comparative dullness of imagination" (p. 371). A. C. Bradley, *Shakespearean Tragedy*, London, 1950. First published 1904.

Chapter 7

Edmund, Goneril, and Regan

Edmund in *King Lear* appears in the first scene of the play in an exchange between his father and the Earl of Kent, in which his bastardy is jokingly presented. Gloucester says:

> Though this knave came something saucily to the world before he was sent for,
> yet was his mother fair, there was good sport at his making, and the whoreson
> must be acknowledged. (20–23)

I think it is important that Edmund's bastardy is insisted on so early in the play. There is a popular belief that bastards are free spirits who are not bound by the social restrictions of legitimate sons.

We feel that the basis for Edmund in *King Lear* is already evident in Philip Faulconbridge, the bastard son of Cordelion, King Richard I, John Faulconbridge's older brother in *King John*. The Bastard is a heroic protagonist of that play, who speaks in the swaggering language of political opportunists. He is called Bastard in the speech prefixes, and he insists on his bastardy as a proof of his "mounting spirit" (1.1.206):

> Who dares not stir by day must walk by night,
> And have is have, however men do catch.
> Near or far off, well won is still well shot,
> And I am I, howe'er I was begot. (172–75)

The Bastard's bravado in *King John* is recalled and expanded in Edmund's long soliloquy in Act I, scene ii of *King Lear*. He is Gloucester's "natural" son—a synonym for bastard—so that it comes as no surprise when he begins by invoking Nature as his goddess and questions the low status of illegitimate sons:

Why bastard? Wherefore base?
When my dimensions are as well compact,
My mind as generous and my shape as true
As honest madam's issue? Why brand they us
With base? With baseness, bastardy? Base, base?
Who in the lusty stealth of nature take
More composition and fierce quality
Than doth within a dull stale tired bed
Go to the creating of a whole tribe of fops
Got 'tween a sleep and wake. (6–15)

Edmund is echoing his father's speech in the previous scene, and he dwells lovingly on the words "base," "baseness," and "bastardy."

Edmund also has strong filiations with Iago in *Othello* in his histrionic skill, in his wit, and in his use of many soliloquies in the early scenes to emphasize his close reliance on the good will of the audience.[1] Some of Edmund's phrasing seems to come right out of *Othello*. For example, his "auricular assurance" (92) echoes Othello's "ocular proof" (3.3.357). But more important than verbal echoes is the fact that Edmund's villainy seems to be modeled on Iago's. In his second soliloquy in Act I, scene ii, Edmund scoffs at Gloucester's idea about astrological influences on human actions. To Edmund everything that happens depends on our will:

An admirable evasion of whoremaster man, to lay his goatish disposition on the charge of a star. My father compounded with my mother under the dragon's tail and my nativity was under Ursa Major, so that it follows I am rough and lecherous. Fut! I should have been that I am had the maidenliest star in the firmament twinkled on my bastardizing. (126–33)

This is what Edmund calls "the excellent foppery of the world" (118); it is remarkably similar to what Iago tells Roderigo:

Virtue? A fig! 'Tis in ourselves that we are thus, or thus. Our bodies are our gardens, to the which our wills are gardeners; so that if we will plant nettles or sow lettuce, set hyssop and weed up thyme . . . why, the power and corrigible authority of this lies in our wills. (*Othello* 1.3.314–17, 320–21)

Edmund's plot against his brother, Edgar, is ruthless, clever, and ingenious. Like Iago, he pretends to be his brother's friend, and, with feigned reluctance he shows his father the invented letter of Edgar. Like the dramatist who is writing *King Lear*, Edmund is a skillful plotter. He speaks in the language of the theater to announce his brother's entrance:

Pat he comes, like the catastrophe of the old comedy. My cue is villainous
melancholy, with a sigh like Tom o'Bedlam. (1.2.134–36)

Notice that Edmund predicts the disguised role his brother takes to escape
pursuit.

In his third and final soliloquy in this scene, Edmund, again like Iago and
other Shakespearean villains, gloats over how easy it is to trick both his father
and his brother:

A credulous father and a brother noble,
Whose nature is so far from doing harms
That he suspects none—on whose foolish honesty
My practices ride easy. (177–80)

Here is again that villain's word "practices," meaning stratagems or tricks,
and we remember how Iago delights in his reputation for honesty. This is
also the case in Antony's oration in *Julius Caesar*: "Brutus is an honorable
man,/ So are they all, all honorable men" (3.2.84–85). Edgar's "foolish honesty" matches Gloucester's credulousness in making them easy victims of
Edmund's plots. His soliloquy ends with a ringing couplet:

Let me, if not by birth, have lands by wit;
All with me's meet that I can fashion fit. (181–82)

Bastards depend on wit and self-fashioning, not on their birth.

Edmund's clever plot is continued with renewed vigor and a reliance on
theatrical tricks in Act II, scene i. Edmund is so naturalistic in his acting that
he goes so far as to cut himself, as if he were stabbed by Edgar:

Some blood drawn on me would beget opinion
Of my more fierce endeavour. I have seen drunkards
Do more than this in sport. (34–36)

But Edmund can learn, even from drunkards, how to give the appearance
of valor. What's interesting about this scene is how fully Edmund imagines
the drama, including imaginary dialogue spoken by his brother. He takes
pleasure in hearing his father call Edgar a "strange and fastened villain" (77),
"fastened" meaning confirmed or inveterate. Edmund obviously delights in
his little playlet. And when Regan asks whether Edgar wasn't "companion
with the riotous knights/ That tended upon my father?" (94–95), Edmund is
pleased to agree: "Yes, madam, he was of that consort" (97). It is all part of
his fertile and self-interested fantasy.

It comes as no surprise that Cornwall should conceive an immediate liking for Edmund:

> Whose virtue and obedience doth this instant
> So much commend itself, you shall be ours.
> Natures of such deep trust we shall much need;
> You we first seize on. (114–17)

Villains seem to have an instantaneous attraction for each other. In a brief soliloquy at the end of Act III, scene iii, Edmund has no scruples about betraying his father, who has received a letter, presumably from Cordelia, who is invading England with her husband, the King of France.

Cornwall will also be informed about Gloucester's help to Lear:

> This seems a fair deserving and must draw me
> That which my father loses, no less than all.
> The younger rises when the old doth fall. (22–24)

Ironically, Edmund is acting out the conspiratorial letter he imagines for Edgar in Act II, scene i. He develops this letter further to make Edgar seem to be in league with the invaders of England, "an intelligent party to the advantages of France" (3.5.11–12). Edmund is suddenly made Earl of Gloucester by Cornwall, and he persists in his duplicity, as if there were a real conflict between his loyalty to Cornwall and his blood ties to his father. Cornwall is very satisfied by this proceeding. He proposes that Edmund "shalt find a dear father in my love" (3.5.24–25).

Cornwall is curiously imperceptive when he dismisses Edmund from the intensely cruel scene of the blinding of Gloucester (III,vii): "the revenges we are bound to take upon your traitorous father are not fit for your beholding" (7–9). When both his eyes have been put out, the benighted Gloucester still calls upon his son Edmund to "enkindle all the sparks of nature/ To quit [requite] this horrid act" (85–86). Regan delights in conveying to him the shocking news:

> Out, treacherous villain,
> Thou call'st on him that hates thee. It was he
> That made the overture of thy treasons to us,
> Who is too good to pity thee. (86–89)

Gloucester is now the villain, and he has a sudden recognition of the truth:

> O my follies! Then Edgar was abused?
> Kind Gods, forgive me that and prosper him. (90–91)

The proper conclusion of this scene is in Act IV, scene v, where Regan comments on the dangers of Gloucester's continued existence:

> It was great ignorance, Gloucester's eyes being out,
> To let him live. Where he arrives he moves
> All hearts against us. Edmund, I think, is gone
> In pity of his misery to dispatch
> His nighted life. . . . (11–15)

In Regan's twisted morality, Edmund is going to kill his father "In pity of his misery," as if it were an act of kindness. This is the first glimpse we have of Edmund the killer, although he seemed indifferent earlier to his accused brother's fate. He later sends his Captain to murder King Lear and Cordelia in prison—what the Captain calls "man's work" (5.3.40).

In Act IV, scene ii, we already see Edmund in an entirely different role as the love object of Goneril, who is very sexual in her wooing:

> Ere long you are like to hear—
> If you dare venture in your own behalf—
> A mistress's command. (19–21)

She then gives him a love token, possibly a chain, and switches to the informal second-person "thy" and "thee:"

> Wear this. Spare speech,
> Decline your head. This kiss, if it durst speak,
> Would stretch thy spirits into the air.
> Conceive, and fare thee well. . . . (21–24)

The courtly and well-spoken Edmund says only before he exits: "Yours in the ranks of death" (25).

When Edgar kills Oswald in Act IV, scene vi, he opens a letter Oswald was carrying from Goneril to Edmund importuning him to kill her husband, the Duke of Albany:

> Let our reciprocal vows be remembered. You have many opportunities to cut him
> off. If your will want not, time and place will be fruitfully offered. (257–60)

She addresses Edmund as if he were a hired assassin to "deliver" her "from the loathed warmth" of the marriage bed, "and supply the place for your labour. Your (wife, so I would say)" (262–64). We saw nothing in the play about the "reciprocal vows" between Edmund and Goneril—only Goneril's lustful and homicidal passion.

There is a similar amorous interplay between Edmund and Regan in Act V, scene i. Regan, too, is overtly sexual. She asks Edmund if he loves her sister; he is cagey in his answer: "In honoured love" (9). But Regan presses on with her questions: "But have you never found my brother's way/ To the forfended [forbidden] place?" (10–11). She suspects Edmund of adultery, but he is careful not to answer her questions directly: "That thought abuses you" (11) and "Fear me not—" (16).

Edmund's long soliloquy at the end of this scene makes it clear that he intends to marry neither sister:

> To both these sisters have I sworn my love,
> Each jealous of the other as the stung
> Are of the adder. Which of them shall I take?
> Both? One? Or neither? Neither can be enjoyed
> If both remain alive. To take the widow
> Exasperates, makes mad her sister Goneril,
> And hardly shall I carry out my side,
> Her husband being alive. (56–63)

This is cold and cynical, like Richard, Duke of Gloucester's, contemptuous wooing of Anne: "I'll have her, but I will not keep her long" (*Richard III* 1.2.229). Edmund's soliloquies vividly imitate the thought processes of speech. He doesn't want to conceal anything from the audience, which is meant to share in his speculations. At the end of this soliloquy we also learn that he rejects Albany's "mercy" for Lear and Cordelia, whom he plans to murder in prison: "for my state/ Stands on me to defend, not to debate" (69–70).

When Edgar defeats Edmund in single combat in Act V, scene iii, there is a definite softening in Edmund's cruel and hard-hearted villainy. To Albany he acknowledges his guilt:

> What you have charged me with, that have I done,
> And more, much more; the time will bring it out.
> 'Tis past and so am I. (160–62)

Edgar desires to "exchange charity" (164) with his brother, as Hamlet does with Laertes, and he asserts the rightness of all that has happened:

> The gods are just and of our pleasant vices
> Make instruments to plague us:
> The dark and vicious place where thee he [Gloucester] got
> Cost him his eyes. (168–71)

Even though this moral formulation seems too neatly balanced, Edmund agrees: "Thou'st spoken right, 'tis true;/The wheel is come full circle, I am here" (171–72). And further: "This speech of yours hath moved me,/And shall perchance do good" (198–99).

The mollification of Edmund continues when he sees the dead bodies of Goneril and Regan:[2]

> Yet Edmund was beloved:
> The one the other poisoned for my sake,
> And after slew herself. (238–40)

This is an uncomfortable moment for Edmund. The violent deaths of Goneril and Regan, neither of whom he intended to marry, is only a proof to him that he "was beloved." It must seem strange to him that anyone could love him at all, since he himself is so much a self-centered creature of will, with no room for anyone else. It is as if both of these women sacrificed themselves for him. Part of Edmund's wonder must be that love exists at all, even in its most pernicious form. This is the first time in the play that he is aware of love as a potent human emotion, and he resembles Iago at this point.

In keeping with Edmund's change of heart, he suddenly remembers the writ he has issued for the secret deaths of Lear and Cordelia in prison: "I pant for life. Some good I mean to do,/Despite of mine own nature" (241–42). The Captain

> hath commission from thy wife [Goneril] and me
> To hang Cordelia in the prison and
> To lay the blame upon her own despair,
> That she fordid herself. (250–53)

At the end of the play Edmund finally recognizes his own evil nature. He tries for some form of reconciliation, but it is too late, and Lear enters right after with the hanged Cordelia in his arms.

Following the Cinderella story, Goneril and Regan are the evil older sisters of Cordelia—*King Lear* is strongly shaped by its folktale origins. They are not obvious villains like Edmund, yet their action in the play in relation to Lear and Gloucester is extraordinarily cruel and villainous. When Regan and her sister shut their doors on Lear and leave him out on the heath in the midst of a furious storm (II, ii), they are clearly indifferent as to whether their old father will manage to survive. We have already spoken of their adulterous love for Edmund, which is never reciprocated. From the first act of the play they are already in league against their old father. Their love speeches are formulaic and rhetorical, like King Claudius's opening oration in *Hamlet*. They speak what King Lear expects to hear from them. Their conversation at the end of this first scene prepares us for the evil that is to follow. They act in concert from the very beginning of the play, as Goneril tells us: "let us hit together" (304–5), or agree jointly. Their insight into their geriatric father is acute. Goneril notes:

> You see how full of changes his age is. The observation we have made of
> it hath not been little. He always loved our sister most, and with what poor
> judgement he hath now cast her off appears too grossly. (290–93)

Regan then generalizes on what becomes the basis for Lear's tragedy: "'Tis the infirmity of his age, yet he hath ever but slenderly known himself" (294–95). So the sisters have a plan, which looks as if it were a conspiracy, about how to deal with their almost senile father.

By Act I, scene iii, their stratagem is already at work. Goneril directs her steward, Oswald, to "come slack of former services" (10) and "Put on what weary negligence you please" (12). She infantilizes her father (as the Fool will shortly emphasize):

> Idle old man,
> That still would manage those authorities
> That he hath given away. Now by my life
> Old fools are babes again and must be used
> With checks as flatteries, when they are seen abused. (18–21)

"Idle" means both indolent and foolish. I think it is important to remember that Goneril and Regan plot against their father from the beginning of the play. As audience, we are not, I think, meant to affirm that what the daughters say is based on observation of Lear and his hundred knights, as these early scenes are often played. Goneril and Regan are emphatically not reasonable, rational creatures responding to a bad domestic situation, as if this were a naturalistic play by Ibsen.

The point is further developed in Act I, scene iv by Goneril's insistent attack on Lear, his Fool, and his knights:

> Not only, sir, this your all-licensed fool,
> But other of your insolent retinue
> Do hourly carp and quarrel, breaking forth
> In rank and not to be endured riots. (191–94)

I think what is involved here is whether Goneril is reporting what we in the audience actually see or whether it is all part of her and her sister's plot against their father.

Goneril initiates her plan by boldly criticizing Lear and his companions:

As you are old and reverend, should be wise.
Here do you keep a hundred knights and squires,
Men so disordered, so debauched and bold,
That this our court, infected with their manners,
Shows like a riotous inn. Epicurism and lust
Makes it more like a tavern or a brothel
Than a graced palace. (231–37)

Goneril is already quite openly threatening her father:

Be then desired,
By her that else will take the thing she begs,
A little to disquantity your train,
And the remainders that shall still depend
To be such men as may besort your age,
Which know themselves, and you. (238–243)

We await anxiously for what will happen, but we know already that
the abdicated King is now without any means to stand up to his elder
daughters.

In Act II, scene ii, Cornwall, the husband of Regan, joins the attack on
Lear. The fact that his messenger, Kent, is put in the stocks is a further insult
to the old King. Cornwall is contemptuous: "This is a fellow of the selfsame
colour/ Our sister [sister-in-law Goneril] speaks of" (135–36)—an additional
proof that all three are plotting together. This scene anticipates the blinding
of Gloucester in Act III, scene vii because we have a strikingly cruel remark
of Regan. When Cornwall decrees that Kent shall sit in the stocks "till noon"
(131), Regan goes him one better: "Till noon? Till night, my lord, and all
night too" (132).

We hear Regan in this scene echoing her sister in their attempt to bargain
away Lear's status:

What, fifty followers?
Is it not well? What should you need of more?
Yea, or so many, sith that both charge and danger
Speak 'gainst so great a number? (426–29)

Goneril backs up her sister:

Why might not you, my lord, receive attendance
From those that she calls servants or from mine? (432–33)

Regan continues to chip away at the initial stipulations:

Why not, my lord? If then they chanced to slack ye
We could control them. If you will come to me—
For now I spy a danger—I entreat you
To bring but five and twenty: to no more
Will I give place or notice. (434–38)

Lear's eloquent "reason not the need" (453) speech is lost on his grasping daughters and Cornwall.

By Act III, scene vi the mad Lear is arraigning his daughters, and this scene serves as a prelude to the blinding of Gloucester in the next scene. First, Goneril, who "kicked the poor King her father" (47–48), then Regan:

let them anatomize Regan; see what breeds about her heart. Is there any
cause in nature that make these hard hearts? (73–74)

Lear is despairing at this point because there is nothing he can do to defend himself.

The scene then shifts to Gloucester, who is captured in III, vii. Regan plays a particularly savage role in this unimaginably cruel scene. When Cornwall orders that Gloucester be bound, Regan goes him one better and says: "Hard, hard. O, filthy traitor!" (32). What has Gloucester ever done to Regan to deserve such treatment? Then Regan plucks his white beard, an insulting act often depicted in martyrdoms. The pinioned Gloucester can only protest:

Naughty lady,
These hairs which thou dost ravish from my chin
Will quicken [come alive] and accuse thee. I am your host. . . . (37–39)

"Naughty" means wicked, a much stronger word in Shakespeare's time than in ours. Earlier, Lear had said to Regan:

Thy sister's naught. O, Regan, she hath tied
Sharp-toothed unkindness, like a vulture, here [pointing to his heart]. (2.2.323–24)

In III,vii the blinding of Gloucester, each eye done separately, emerges as an improvised punishment suggested by his own response to Regan about why he has accompanied the lunatic King to Dover:

Because I would not see thy cruel nails
Pluck out his poor old eyes; nor thy fierce sister
In his anointed flesh stick boarish fangs. (55–57)

This statement immediately prompts Cornwall to say:

> See't shalt thou never. Fellows, hold the chair;
> Upon these eyes of thine I'll set my foot. (66–67)

We know from Regan's rejoinder that Cornwall has only stamped out one eye: "One side will mock another—th'other too" (70). The physical cruelty of this scene is amplified by the fact that Gloucester's two eyes are separately extinguished.

When Regan stabs to death the servant who has mortally wounded her husband, the servant's dying lines are spoken to Gloucester:

> O, I am slain. My lord, you have one eye left
> To see some mischief on him. (80–81)

Cornwall immediately seizes the occasion to pluck out Gloucester's remaining eye: "Lest it see more, prevent it. Out, vile jelly,/ Where is thy lustre now?" (82–83). Then Regan directs a servant to thrust Gloucester "out at gates and let him smell/ His way to Dover" (92–93). The horror of the scene comes from its insistence on intolerable physical details.

We have already discussed the way Goneril and Regan openly woo Edmund. It is all very sexual, as Goneril says contemptuously to Edmund:

> O, the difference of man and man!
> To thee a woman's services are due;
> A fool usurps my bed. (4.2.26–28)

Kent calls Goneril and Regan "dog-hearted daughters" (4.3.46), which continues the persistently negative connotations for dogs in Shakespeare. At the end of the play, the daughters vie with each other for possession of Edmund, who is singularly indifferent to both. Goneril poisons Regan, and Regan kills herself with a knife. Edmund confesses that he "was contracted to them" (5.3.227), but he expresses no personal sorrow at their deaths. He is only flattered, in an almost incredulous way, that he "was beloved" (238). Albany sees the tragic events as a "judgement of the heavens that makes us tremble" (230), but he insists that it "Touches us not with pity" (231). The deaths of the evil daughters seem like a providential element in the play, but very soon we see the dead Cordelia in Lear's arms. The mystery of the tragedy in *King Lear* may be better formulated in Cordelia's words at the beginning of this scene: "We are not the first/ Who with best meaning have incurred the worst" (3–4).

Edmund is a cunning villain, like Iago and Richard, Duke of Gloucester. It is emphasized that he is a bastard, like Faulconbridge in *King John*, and therefore a free and natural spirit, a creature of strong will, who is also an atheist. He scoffs at his father's astrological belief in the influence of the stars. He seems to be tickled by the idea that he is beloved by both Goneril and Regan, who kill themselves for his sake, but he himself is incapable of loving either of them or anyone else. Without much scruple, he betrays his father to Cornwall and is ambitious to rise in fortune. Goneril and Regan are not exactly villains, but they plot against their aging father from the beginning of the play. They are determined to reduce his status, especially in regard to his hundred knights, but when they leave him out on the heath during a furious storm, they don't care whether he lives or dies. Cornwall, the husband of Regan, participates in one of the cruelest scenes in Shakespeare—the blinding of Gloucester—and Regan thinks later in the play that they would have been better off had they killed Gloucester.

NOTES

1. See Robert Bechtold Heilman's detailed and comprehensive study, *This Great Stage: Image and Structure in King Lear*, Baton Rouge, LA: Louisiana State University Press, 1948.

2. See Christina León Alfar, *Fantasies of Female Evil: The Dynamics of Gender and Power in Shakesperean Tragedy*, Newark, DE: University of Delaware Press, 2003, especially Chapter 3, "Looking for Goneril and Regan."

Chapter 8

Angelo

Angelo in *Measure for Measure* is an extreme character. He represents, like a person in a morality play, a claim to extreme virtue, which turns suddenly to extreme vice. He is clearly marked as a villain because he intends to kill Claudio, in spite of his agreement with Isabella (although she doesn't really keep her part of the bargain either). He is made to believe that Claudio's head has been cut off in the prison and sent to him. Like Tybalt in *Romeo and Juliet,* he is absolutely humorless and doesn't indulge in the sort of histrionic flourishes characteristic of Aaron, Richard III, or Iago. He does, however, have many soliloquies in which he tries to win the sympathy of the audience.

Measure for Measure is an unusual play, a tragicomedy, often classified as a problem play. It has an unusually large number of reflective speeches on abstract issues about ethics, morality, and politics. For example, the play begins with the testing of Angelo. This is puzzling because the Duke has already appointed him to rule in Vienna in his place. The Duke clearly knows of Angelo's duplicity in not marrying Mariana, as he tells Isabella in Act III, scene i:

> She should this Angelo have married; was affianced to her by oath, and the nuptial appointed: between which time of the contract and limit of the solemnity, her brother Frederick was wracked at sea, having in that perished vessel the dowry of his sister. But mark how heavily this befell to the poor gentlewoman: there she lost a noble and renowned brother, in his love toward her ever most kind and natural; with him, the portion and sinew of her fortune, her marriage dowry; with both, her combinate [betrothed] husband, this well-seeming Angelo. (216–27)

Notice that although we are only in the middle of the play, the Duke is already speaking of Angelo as "well-seeming," a creature of false appearances. He is adamant and deceptive in his rejection of Mariana, which is clearly a matter of money (the loss of her dowry).

In the Duke's description, Angelo is represented as heartlessly cruel:

> Left her in her tears, and dried not one of them with his comfort; swallowed his vows whole, pretending in her discoveries of dishonor: in few, bestowed her on her own lamentation, which she yet wears for his sake; and he, a marble to her tears, is washed with them, but relents not. (229–34)

Angelo invents discoveries of Mariana's dishonor—in other words, he slanders her. He is cold, "a marble," and unsympathetic to her suffering.

Meanwhile, the Duke arranges the bed-trick, by which the wronged Mariana shall be substituted for Isabella. This device is intended to solve everyone's difficulties:

> by this, is your brother saved, your honor untainted, the poor Mariana advantaged, and the corrupt deputy scaled. (257–60)

Notice how clearly the Duke judges Angelo. He will be "scaled," in other words, weighed in the scales, an important adjunct of his testing. But despite Angelo's "unjust unkindness" (244–45), Mariana persists in her love for him.

Among the many ambiguities in *Measure for Measure* is this one: why, if the Duke already knows of Angelo's duplicity in dealing with Mariana, does he appoint him to rule in his place in Vienna, and why is there such a strong emphasis on the testing of Angelo in the early scenes? The doubts about Angelo begin almost immediately. The Duke asks Escalus: "What figure of us, think you, he will bear?" (16), and again at the end of his speech: "What think you of it?" (21). Escalus, of course, reassures the Duke that he has made the right choice. It is curious that Angelo himself asks the Duke for further vetting:

> Let there be some more test made of my mettle
> Before so noble and so great a figure
> Be stamped upon it. (48–50)

This is oddly like Isabella's first question when she enters the nunnery: "And have you nuns no farther privileges?" (1.4.1), by which she speaks

> not as desiring more,
> But rather wishing a more strict restraint
> Upon the sisterhood, the votarists of Saint Clare. (3–5)

There is an unusual (and often overlooked) temperamental affinity between Isabella and Angelo.

Angelo's rigor in applying the new law in Vienna falls immediately on Claudio, who is condemned to death for getting Julietta with child without the proper form of marriage. Again, doubts are raised about Angelo's "tyranny" (1.2.166). He

Awakes me all the enrollèd penalties
Which have, like unscoured armor, hung by th' wall
So long, that nineteen zodiacs have gone round,
And none of them been worn; and, for a name,
Now puts the drowsy and neglected act
Freshly on me. 'Tis surely for a name. (169–74)

It is interesting that Claudio raises the point (and repeats it) that Angelo may be punishing him severely merely to promote his own reputation—"for a name"—rather than for any legitimate legal or political reason.

In the next scene (I, iii) the Duke makes his purposes explicit. He knows Angelo to be "A man of stricture and firm abstinence" (12). This is the only use of "stricture" in Shakespeare, and it seems to refer to Angelo's self-repression rather than to his strictness to others. The Duke will disguise himself as a friar "to behold" Angelo's "sway" (43), in his role as the Duke's hatchet man. The testing function is strongly established at the end of the scene, where the Duke sets out binary opposites:

Lord Angelo is precise,
Stands at a guard with envy [malice]; scarce confesses
That his blood flows, or that his appetite
Is more to bread than stone. Hence shall we see,
If power change purpose, what our seemers be. (50–54)

"Precise" is a word specifically associated with the Puritans in the sixteenth and seventeenth centuries, referring to their literal interpretation of the Bible and their pharisaical over-scrupulousness in religious observance ("Precisian" is a synonym for Puritan). Remember that in Act III, scene i, the Duke spoke of Angelo as "well-seeming" (227).

In the Duke's speech, blood is not only the seat of the emotions, but in Renaissance physiology it was also thought to carry the sexual impulses. This is at the heart of the play, since Angelo's sexual appetite overcomes his strict morality. Throughout, however, he is thought to be cold, unfeeling, and unemotional. As the Duke notes, Angelo hardly admits that "his blood flows," or that he experiences sexual desire. He is stone-like ("marble" in 3.1.233) and denies having any appetite, or sexual feelings. That is the impression he wishes to convey.

In the next scene (I, iv) we have Lucio's more detailed character sketch of Lord Angelo,

> a man whose blood
> Is very snow-broth; one who never feels
> The wanton stings and motions of the sense,
> But doth rebate [make dull] and blunt his natural edge
> With profits of the mind, study and fast. (57–61)

We are not surprised that Lucio, a satirical speaker, thinks Angelo a hypocrite, a conclusion that the audience will realize very soon. "Sense" is an important sexual word that marks Angelo's temptation and fall in Act II, scene ii. As he confesses in an aside, Isabella "speaks, and 'tis/ Such sense, that my sense breeds with it" (141–42). "Edge" (60) is also a sexual word referring to keenness of desire.

Lucio presents himself to the Duke as an expert on Angelo. In Act III, scene ii he declares that the deputy "was not made by man and woman after this downright way of creation" (106–8), in other words by sexual intercourse. Lucio testifies to Angelo's public image as a cold, sexless creature:

> Some report a sea maid [mermaid] spawned him; some, that he was begot
> between two stockfishes [dried and salted cod]. But it is certain that when
> he makes water his urine is congealed ice; that I know to be true. And he is
> a motion [puppet] generative; that's infallible. (110–14)

Of course, Lucio means to stress Angelo's hypocrisy and to counter his attempt to extirpate sexuality in Vienna.

By the time of this scene, the Duke seems already to have judged his deputy, but he lets the action play itself out. We appear to be beyond the testing phase when the Duke declares:

> If his own life answer the straitness of his proceeding, it shall become him
> well; wherein if he chance to fail, he hath sentenced himself. (258–60)

This idea is expanded in the Duke's didactic soliloquy (in tetrameter couplets) at the end of the scene:

> Twice treble shame on Angelo,
> To weed my vice and let his grow.
> O, what may man within him hide,
> Though angel on the outward side! (272–75)

In his function as moral overlord of the play, the Duke readies himself to fulfill his purpose: "Craft against vice I must apply" (280). Angelo's villainous motives are no longer in question: he is identified here as "vice."

Like other Shakespearean villains, we see the "stern" (66) Angelo asserting his absolute will in Act II, scene ii. Isabella pleads for her brother's life: "I do think that you might pardon him,/ And neither heaven nor man grieve at the mercy" (49–50), but Angelo is implacable: "I will not do't." Isabella asks again: "But can you, if you would?" (51) Angelo's answer seems to end the discussion: "Look what I will not, that I cannot do" (52). Isabella, however, persists:

But might you do't, and do the world no wrong,
If so your heart were touched with that remorse [compassion]
As mine is to him? (53–55)

Angelo's answer falsely shifts the responsibility for Claudio's death from his own adamant will to the impersonal institution of law and justice: "He's sentenced; 'tis too late" (55). Some lines further, Angelo says the same thing more explicitly: "It is the law, not I, condemn your brother" (80).

Angelo's determination cracks at line 141, when he admits that he is personally moved not only by the good sense of Isabella's theological arguments, but even more importunately by the sensuality of Isabella herself: "She speaks, and 'tis/ Such sense, that my sense breeds with it." In his long soliloquy at the end of this scene, Angelo, like Claudius in *Hamlet*, is fully aware of his own guilt, which, by the direct address of soliloquy, he shares with the audience:

What's this? What's this? Is this her fault or mine?
Ha, not she. Nor doth she tempt: but it is I
That, lying by the violet in the sun,
Do as the carrion does, not as the flow'r,
Corrupt with virtuous season. (161–67)

Isabella is the violet, the flower brought to blossom by the energy of the sun's beams, which also putrefy the carrion, or dead body, represented by Angelo. He is suddenly remarkably insightful, and his style shifts to a more relaxed and less formal colloquial. Angelo never mitigates his own acute sense of wrongdoing, but he does elevate himself to sainthood (as he does Isabella) by making his temptation irresistible: "O cunning enemy, that, to catch a saint,/ With saints dost bait thy hook!" (179–80). He is caught in his own paradoxes, sinning "in loving virtue" (182). He doesn't mitigate his guilt, but he disguises his carnality in moral casuistry.

By Act II, scene iv, Angelo is strongly aware of the power of his "blood," or desire, from which he cannot escape. He doesn't speak directly of conscience, like Claudius in *Hamlet*, but he is troubled by the extreme dualism that overwhelms him, as is seen in his opening soliloquy:

When I would pray and think, I think and pray
To several subjects: heaven hath my empty words,
Whilst my invention [imagination], hearing not my tongue,
Anchors on Isabel: heaven in my mouth,
As if I did but only chew his name,
And in my heart the strong and swelling evil
Of my conception. (1–7)

In his dilemma, Angelo suddenly becomes a vivid speaker, who only "chews" on God's name.

But Angelo's intellectual and theological debate doesn't continue for very long. Soon he is focused on his imperious sexual demands: that Isabella "Give up your body to such sweet uncleanness/ As she that he hath stained" (54–55). Presumably, Angelo is referring to Claudio and Juliet, but the euphemism "sweet uncleanness" already strikes a false note, as does his proposition that there is "a charity in sin/ To save this brother's life" (63–64). Gradually, Angelo becomes more imperious in his speech, and more sexist, too, as he insists that Isabella put on "the destined livery" (138) of a woman and submit to male and patriarchal desire.

By the time of his last speech in this scene, Angelo has become more direct and villainous. He is sure that no one will believe Isabella:

My unsoiled name, th' austereness of my life,
My vouch against you, and my place i' th' state,
Will so your accusation overweigh,
That you shall stifle in your own report,
And smell of calumny. (155–59)

So Isabella is blocked, and Angelo can now "give my sensual race the rein" (160). Again, he emphasizes that it is all a matter of will. If she denies "yielding up thy body to my will" (164), Angelo threatens to condemn Claudio "To ling'ring sufferance" (167), in other words, to torture him and "prove a tyrant to him" (169).

The upshot of these highly sexual scenes comes in Act IV, scene iv, when there is a strong rumor of the Duke's return. Angelo is worried. He feels guilty about what he has done, since he believes that he has had intercourse with Isabella and that her brother has been executed at his command. In a soliloquy at the end of this scene, he reflects on his evil deeds:

A deflow'red maid,
And by an eminent body that enforced

The law against it! But that her tender shame
Will not proclaim against her maiden loss,
How might she tongue me! (23–27)

But he is sure that his "authority" (28) will protect him.
About Claudio he feels conflicted:

He should have lived,
Save that his riotous youth, with dangerous sense,
Might in the times to come have ta'en revenge,
By so receiving a dishonored life
With ransom of such shame. Would yet he had lived! (30–34)

Angelo invents Claudio's "riotous youth," about which we hear nothing in the play. Also, he attributes to Claudio a "dangerous sense" that is more appropriate to himself.

Angelo's couplet conclusion is already a judgment on himself and his transgressions:

Alack, when once our grace we have forgot,
Nothing goes right; we would, and we would not. (35–36)

He is well aware that he has fallen from "grace." At the end of the play, he requests an immediate sentence of death from the Duke, whom he speaks of in theological terms: "When I perceive your Grace, like pow'r divine,/ Hath looked upon my passes" (5.1.372–73). But *Measure for Measure* is, after all, a tragicomedy, so that Angelo can be married to the long-faithful Mariana of the moated grange and be pardoned by the merciful Duke.

Angelo is a different kind of villain from any we have encountered thus far. He is the super virtuous man who turns out to be rotten inside. Angelo's burning desire to have sex with Isabella, the novice of St. Clare at the beginning of the play, is granted with the understanding that her brother Claudio will be spared from death. But Angelo wants to have it both ways. He presses for Claudio's execution even as he pursues his tryst with Isabella. Angelo is made to believe that his commands have been carried out and that he has enjoyed Isabella. Of course, neither is true. Remember that Angelo is a villain in a comedy, and at the end, even though the play is called *Measure for Measure*, everyone is pardoned. Angelo is like the villains of the tragedies and the history plays until the bed trick, by which the Duke ingeniously has Angelo sleep with his betrothed wife, Mariana of the moated grange, whom he will marry in the happy ending.

Chapter 9

Tybalt

Tybalt in *Romeo and Juliet* has all the characteristics of a villain, but he is rather different from the villains we have been discussing thus far: he is a caricature of a swordsman in the mode of the Italian dueling manuals. Tybalt is not particularly jocular or histrionic like other Shakespearean villains. He is, in fact, so deadly serious as to be a parody of a villain. He speaks in an affected style, like Osric in *Hamlet*. Like most of Shakespeare's villains, Tybalt is immediately ready to kill if the need presents itself. He does indeed kill Mercutio, treacherously (it would appear) under Romeo's arm. He returns with the clear intent to kill Romeo.

Tybalt is not a major character in *Romeo and Juliet*, but he serves as an important catalyst for the tragic action.[1] He is Lady Capulet's nephew. When Tybalt enters in the first scene of the play, Benvolio is already trying to end the swordplay between the servants of the Montagues and the Capulets: "Part, fools!/ Put up your swords. You know not what you do" (66–67). Tybalt's first words are in the blustering rodomontade of the professional swordsman:

What, art thou drawn among these heartless hinds [rustics]?
Turn thee, Benvolio; look upon thy death. (68–69)

Tybalt always speaks with rhetorical bravado, as if he were an anticipation of Pistol in the *Henry IV* plays. His speech is mannered and affected, verging on the comic.

His elevated, emotional style, sharply removed from ordinary conversation, is continued in his second speech:

What, drawn, and talk of peace? I hate the word
As I hate hell, all Montagues, and thee.
Have at thee, coward! (72–74)

Tybalt embodies the mindless feud between the Capulets and the Montagues, whose origin is never revealed. Everyone in the play, including his uncle Capulet, thinks of him as a somewhat ridiculous figure.

In Benvolio's account of the quarrel to old Montague, there is more than a touch of amusement at the exaggerated gestures and language of Tybalt:

Here were the servants of your adversary
And yours, close fighting ere I did approach.
I drew to part them. In the instant came
The fiery Tybalt, with his sword prepared;
Which, as he breathed defiance to my ears,
He swung about his head and cut the winds,
Who, nothing hurt withal, hissed him in scorn. (109–15)

Here is a familiar acting metaphor to underscore Tybalt's histrionic gesture—the wind created by his thrusts is personified and hisses the "fiery Tybalt" to scorn. The image anticipates the "rugged" Pyrrhus in the *Dido and Aeneas* play in *Hamlet*. Remember what the Player recites with such high drama:

Pyrrhus at Priam drives, in rage strikes wide,
But with the whiff and wind of his fell sword
Th' unnervèd father falls. (2.2.483–85)

Tybalt and Pyrrhus, as archetypal swordsmen, both overact badly, although Pyrrhus in *Hamlet* has no lines and therefore no rhetorical flourishes.

The same sense of Tybalt as a foolish blusterer is more fully developed in Act I, scene v, during the ball the Capulets are giving, at which Romeo encounters Juliet. Tybalt's provocative violence is linked with Romeo's falling in love at first sight with Juliet:

Did my heart love till now? Forswear it, sight!
For I ne'er saw true beauty till this night. (54–55)

Then Tybalt expresses his discordant and homicidal indignation:

This, by his voice, should be a Montague.
Fetch me my rapier, boy. What! Dares the slave
Come hither, covered with an antic face [mask],
To fleer [jeer] and scorn at our solemnity? (56–59)

Of course, we know that Romeo's fleering and scorning is all a product of Tybalt's inflamed imagination—we have just listened to his extraordinary love speech beginning "O, she doth teach the torches to burn bright!" (46). Tybalt is at the heart of the feud, which seems otherwise to be winding down, and, until Tybalt kills Mercutio, *Romeo and Juliet* seems much more like a romantic comedy than a tragedy. But here Tybalt answers Romeo's lyric couplets with a couplet of his own:

Now, by the stock and honor of my kin,
To strike him dead I hold it not a sin. (60–61)

This is a true villain's declaration.

The elder Capulet rebukes his nephew for being completely out of keeping with the merriment: "Why, how now, kinsman? Wherefore storm you so?" (62). "Storm" and other descriptive words that Capulet uses give us a good indication of how Shakespeare expected Tybalt to play his part. He is an absurdly inappropriate figure, but his uncle speaks to him as if he were also very young and impetuous. He advises him to "be patient" (73) and "put off these frowns" (75) because even though Romeo is a Montague, he is also "a virtuous and well-governed youth" (70). But Tybalt is testy: "I'll not endure him" (78).

We see Capulet growing angry with his nephew, and upbraiding him with energetically colloquial speech:

He shall be endured.
What, goodman boy! I say he shall. Go to!
Am I the master here, or you? Go to!
You'll not endure him, God shall mend my soul!
You'll make a mutiny among my guests!
You will set cock-a-hoop [topsy-turvy]. You'll be the man! (78–83)

We hear a similarly vigorous colloquial when Capulet excoriates his daughter for not wanting to marry Paris (III,v).

In the scene of the ball, Capulet grows increasingly impatient with his nephew and calls him "saucy boy" (1.5.85) and "princox" (88), a strong word for impertinence and disrespect for one's elders. This is the only use of "princox" in Shakespeare, which the *Oxford English Dictionary* defines as "A pert, forward, saucy boy or youth; a conceited young fellow; a coxcomb." This applies very well to Tybalt, who is untouched by all of these imprecations and ends with two ominous couplets:

Patience perforce with willful choler meeting
Makes my flesh tremble in their different greeting.

I will withdraw; but this intrusion shall,
Now seeming sweet, convert to bitt'rest gall. (91–94)

This is followed immediately by Romeo and Juliet's interactive love sonnet, beginning with Romeo's "If I profane with my unworthiest hand" (95).
Shakespeare is experimenting with abrupt contrast, with Romeo's intense
love speeches set against Tybalt's blustering.

In answer to Benvolio's question, "Why, what is Tybalt?" (18), Mercutio
goes to great lengths in Act II, scene iv to characterize him:

> More than Prince of Cats. O, he's the courageous captain of compliments.
> He fights as you sing pricksong—keeps time, distance, and proportion;
> he rests his minim rests, one, two, and the third in your bosom! The very butcher
> of a silk button, a duelist, a duelist! A gentleman of the very first house, of the first
> and second cause. Ah, the immortal *passado!* The *punto reverso!* The hay! (19–27)

It's interesting that Tybalt is the "Prince of Cats," recalling Tybert the prince
of cats in the medieval tales of Reynard the Fox. A tabby cat is usually female
and striped as contrasted with a male tom cat. Is Tib a familiar name for a
female cat?

In any case, Mercutio continues his satirical portrait that makes Tybalt look
and speak like the affected Osric in *Hamlet*:

> The pox of such antic, lisping, affecting fantasticoes—these new tuners of
> accent! "By Jesu, a very good blade! A very tall man! A very good whore!"
> Why, is not this a lamentable thing, grandsire, that we should be thus afflicted
> with these strange flies, these fashionmongers, these pardon-me's, who stand so
> much on the new form that they cannot sit at ease on the old bench? O, their
> bones, their bones! (29–37)

There is a pun on "bones" and the French *bon*, with a possible allusion to
the "bone-ache," which is a word for venereal disease, the French malady.[2]
Mercutio is enjoying himself by representing Tybalt as a foppish duelist,
who sticks to all the punctilios of the dueling manuals. He also imitates
the fashionable Tybalt's affected speech and jokes about the way that he is
dressed.

Mercutio's long speech about duelling by the book recalls the conversation
of Touchstone and Jaques in *As You Like It* about the precise etiquette of the
duel. Touchstone expatiates about how to manage a quarrel according to the
many manuals, chiefly Italian, that were being published at the time:

> O sir, we quarrel in print, by the book, as you have books for good manners.
> I will name you the degrees. The first, the Retort Courteous; the second, the

Quip Modest; the third, the Reply Churlish. . . . All these you may avoid but the
Lie Direct, and you may avoid that too, with an If. (5.4.90–94, 96–98)

Jaques and the Duke applaud Touchstone's performance. Duke Senior says:
"He uses his folly like a stalking horse, and under the presentation of that he
shoots his wit" (106–7).

Unlike other joking villains in Shakespeare, Tybalt is profoundly serious
about being a swordsman ready to kill. More than anyone else in the play,
he represents the deadly intensity of the feud between the houses, a feud we
learn nothing about. By Act III, scene i, Tybalt is ready to kill someone, especially Romeo, whom he calls "a villain" (62). But Romeo forswears fighting
since he feels allied to the Capulets by his love for Juliet. This angers the
testy Mercutio:

O calm, dishonorable, vile submission!
Alla stoccata carries it away.
Tybalt, you ratcatcher, will you walk? (74–76)

Again, Tybalt is the cat, Mr. *alla stoccata*, a term for a thrust in the Italian
fencing manuals.

Mercutio always refers to Tybalt as a ridiculous figure, a foppish swordsman. In answer to his "What wouldst thou have with me?" (77), Mercutio
persists in the cat imagery:

Good King of Cats, nothing but one of your nine lives. That I mean to make
bold withal, and, as you shall use me hereafter, dry-beat the rest of the eight.
(78–81)

When they fight, Tybalt *"under Romeo's arm thrusts Mercutio in"* (91 s.d.),
as the stage direction of Quarto 1 reads.[3] He is mortally wounded, but he
continues with the cat imagery. He only has "a scratch, a scratch. Marry, 'tis
enough" (93–94). He is astounded that such an absurd figure as Tybalt should
have been able to kill him:

Zounds, a dog, a rat, a mouse, a cat, to scratch a man to death! A braggart, a
rogue, a villain, that fights by the book of arithmetic! Why the devil came you
between us? I was hurt under your arm. (101–5)

It is important to remember that, I think, Mercutio is killed by stealth and
guile while he is sheltered under Romeo's arm, who is trying to stop the
quarrel. This also identifies Tybalt as a villain, who will do anything to murder his opponent. He is like Achilles in *Troilus and Cressida* who, with his
Myrmidons, slaughters the unarmed Hector (V,viii). He is also like Aufidius

in *Coriolanus*, who, early in the play, vows to kill Marcius whatever way offers itself: "I'll potch at him some way,/ Or wrath or craft may get him" (1.10.15–16). This is the only use of "potch" in Shakespeare, a colloquial or slang word not in the *Oxford English Dictionary*, meaning to thrust or poke. Aufidius, with his *"three or four Conspirators"* (5.6.8 s.d.), manages to provoke Coriolanus. He not only kills him, but he also stands triumphantly on his dead body (5.6.132 s.d.).

The "furious Tybalt" (3.1.123) returns, now bent on killing Romeo. He is still full of duelist's rhetoric as he taunts him: "Thou, wretched boy, that didst consort him [Mercutio] here,/ Shall with him hence" (132–33). But Romeo quickly kills Tybalt and flees. In Benvolio's report to the Prince, Tybalt is represented as a swordsman who cannot control his "unruly spleen" (159). In Renaissance physiology, the spleen was thought to be the seat of emotions and passions. In Benvolio's account, Tybalt is enraged and always ready to kill. Romeo's pleas about how "nice" (156), or trivial, the quarrel is have no effect on Tybalt; they

> Could not take truce with the unruly spleen
> Of Tybalt deaf to peace, but that he tilts
> With piercing steel at bold Mercutio's breast. . . . (159–61)

Romeo is still trying to end the fighting. He cries "Hold, friends! Friends, part!" (167), "beats down their fatal points,/ And 'twixt them rushes" (168–69). But this is all wrong. When Romeo tries to shield Mercutio by holding him underneath his arm, Tybalt seizes the treacherous opportunity: "An envious thrust from Tybalt hit the life/ Of stout Mercutio" (170–71). "Envious" is a strong word meaning full of ill-will and malice, very different from its modern meaning.

Tybalt is mourned by the Capulets for the rest of the play. The Nurse says:

> O Tybalt, Tybalt, the best friend I had!
> O courteous Tybalt! Honest gentleman! (3.2.61–62)

His death suddenly elevates him. Capulet exclaims that his daughter "loved her kinsman Tybalt dearly,/ And so did I" (3.4.2–3). Lady Capulet assumes that her daughter is weeping for him:

> Evermore weeping for your cousin's death?
> What, wilt thou wash him from his grave with tears?
> And if thou couldst, thou couldst not make him live. (3.5.70–72)

She is eager to take vengeance for her nephew and proposes to poison Romeo in Mantua. It is curious that at this point Juliet, too, wants to participate in the revenge action. We cannot take literally what she says: "Would none but I might venge my cousin's death" (88). In the next scene, Paris reports: "Immoderately she weeps for Tybalt's death" (4.1.6).

In Juliet's long soliloquy at the end of Act IV, scene iii, as she prepares to drink Friar Lawrence's sleeping potion, she is preoccupied with the image of her dead cousin. She has a fearful vision of the tomb in which she shall sleep as if dead: "Where bloody Tybalt, yet but green in earth,/ Lies fest'ring in his shroud" (42–43). She fears that she will become distraught "And pluck the mangled Tybalt from his shroud" (52), and she has a frightening vision of the dead Tybalt looking to take revenge on Romeo:

O, look! Methinks I see my cousin's ghost
Seeking out Romeo, that did spit his body
Upon a rapier's point. Stay, Tybalt, stay! (55–57)

Tybalt is an active presence in Juliet's imagination, and Romeo's killing of him is equivocal. To "spit his body/ Upon a rapier's point" is not a favorable image of Romeo as a swordsman, but she definitely wants to prevent Tybalt's ghost from harming Romeo: "Stay, Tybalt, stay!"

At the very end of the play when Romeo enters the tomb to kill himself, he remembers Tybalt and seems to want to make his peace with him, as Hamlet does with Laertes:

Tybalt, liest thou there in thy bloody sheet?
O, what more favor can I do to thee
Than with that hand that cut thy youth in twain
To sunder his that was thine enemy?
Forgive me, cousin! (5.3.97–101)

Of course, Romeo is not literally Tybalt's cousin, but the term was used generally to indicate a degree of familiarity, intimacy, or friendship (*OED*, sense 5), so that you thought of your cousin as a kinsman. Friar Lawrence, too, speaks of Tybalt's "untimely death" (234). Everyone seems to want to erase the ferocity and bloodiness of the earlier scene (III,i) in which Tybalt kills Mercutio.

Tybalt is one of Shakespeare's least developed villains, who has only a minor role in *Romeo and Juliet*, yet his stabbing of Mercutio is the catalyst for the tragic action in the play. He expresses himself as a caricature of an Italianate swordsman, who strictly follows the dueling manuals of Shakespeare's time. So what are we to make of him? No other Shakespearean villain speaks like Tybalt. He is a parody villain, as Osric in *Hamlet* is a parody courtier. He is almost laughable, yet deadly. He manages, by a trick, to kill Mercutio, then Romeo kills him, so we are forced to take Tybalt seriously as the initiator of the tragedy. But there is heavy irony in the fact that he remains a princox to the end. Among the difficulties of *Romeo and Juliet* as a fully developed tragedy is just this point: that, as Mercutio complains, the ridiculous but deadly Tybalt, the Prince of Cats, can "scratch a man to death" (3.1.101).

NOTES

1. See Susan Snyder, *The Comic Matrix of Shakespeare's Tragedies*, Princeton, NJ: Princeton University Press, 1979, Chapter 2. Snyder has some very perceptive observations about Tybalt, who "alone takes the feud really seriously. It is his inner law, the propeller of his fiery nature" (p. 60).

2. See the note in the Arden edition of *Romeo and Juliet*, ed. Brian Gibbons, London, UK: Methuen, 1980, p. 144.

3. Bernice W. Kliman and Laury Magnus, the editors of the New Kittredge edition of the play, note that this stage direction does not appear in the later quartos. Their edition is part of the Focus series, Newburyport, MA: Focus Publishing, 2008, p. 63.

Chapter 10

Calumniators:

Don John, Iachimo, and Lucio

Don John in *Much Ado About Nothing,* Iachimo in *Cymbeline,* and Lucio in *Measure for Measure*—all characters in comedies—are all calumniators, not villains. They resemble the villains in the tragedies and history plays, however, although their scope of evil-doing is much less extensive. They don't directly bring about anyone's death (except that Hero is reputed to be dead in *Much Ado*), although they do cause a fair amount of perturbation and grief. Their motives are deliberately left vague. In their lack of any serious purpose behind their actions, they seem to fit well with Coleridge's characterization of Iago as the "motive-hunting of motiveless malignity."[1]

Don John is a somewhat anomalous character in *Much Ado About Nothing,* which is a lively comedy focusing on the merry war between Beatrice and Benedick. Don John suffers from melancholy right from the beginning of the play, like Antonio in *The Merchant of Venice,* whose first words are: "In sooth I know not why I am so sad" (1.1.1). We never find out why Antonio is so sad, although there are many speculations, nor do we learn what makes Don John a malcontent. Leonato bids him welcome to Messina and suggests that a quarrel with his brother, Don Pedro, has now been patched up: "being reconciled to the Prince your brother, I owe you all duty" (1.1.150–51). We never learn anything further about this quarrel. Like Edmund in *King Lear* and Faulconbridge in *King John,* Don John is a bastard, which implies that he is a free and independent spirit. Like other malcontents, he is also taciturn, a man "not of many words" (152).[2]

In Act I, scene iii, there is great emphasis on Don John's melancholy disposition, like Jaques in *As You Like It* (but Duke Senior offers an explanation for Jaques's satirical world view). Don John seems to wallow in his incurable sadness, so that his plot against Hero seems to offer a way of cheering himself up. He sets forth, without any explanation, his essential character:

> I cannot hide what I am. I must be sad when I have cause, and smile at no man's jests; eat when I have stomach, and wait for no man's leisure; sleep when I am drowsy, and tend on no man's business; laugh when I am merry, and claw no man in his humor. (12–17)

In other words, like all bastards in Shakespeare, he is self-willed and at liberty to do what he pleases. He will flatter no one (literally, not "claw," or scratch their backs).

Conrade reminds him that he has "of late stood out against your brother, and he hath ta'en you newly into his grace" (19–21). But Don John insists on the prerogatives of an illegimate son. He will not kowtow to his brother regardless of the consequences:

> it better fits my blood to be disdained of all than to fashion a carriage to rob love from any. In this, though I cannot be said to be a flattering man, it must not be denied but I am a plain-dealing villain. (26–30)

This is a remarkable declaration that allies Don John with Aaron, Richard III, Iago, and Edmund. He is plain-dealing in the sense of open and honest (Wycherley called his play of 1677, based on Molière's *Misanthrope, The Plain Dealer*).

Don John boasts of the fact that, as a malcontent, he has no dishonest pretences:

> I am trusted with a muzzle and enfranchised with a clog; therefore I have decreed not to sing in my cage. If I had my mouth, I would bite; if I had my liberty, I would do my liking. In the meantime let me be that I am, and seek not to alter me. (30–35)

These are all tantalizing hints about Don John's character, especially in relation to his brother, but none of them is developed in the play. He is fated to remain an unexplored minor character. When he hears of Claudio's intended marriage to Hero, he immediately seizes on this event as a "model to build mischief on" (44–45). It looks as if Don John is using Claudio to get back at his favored and legitimate brother. He calls Claudio "That young start-up," who has "all the glory of my overthrow" (63–64). Don John's "overthrow" is not stated explicitly, but, presumably, he uses Claudio's marriage as a pretext to attack Don Pedro: "If I can cross him any way, I bless myself every way" (64–65). There is nothing in the play to suggest that Don John has any personal animus against Claudio.

Don John enlists Borachio and pays him well (a thousand ducats) to calumniate Hero and to break up her marriage to Claudio. Borachio boasts of the ill effects of his "proof:" "Proof enough to misuse the Prince, to vex Claudio, to undo Hero, and kill Leonato" (28–29). Don John is pleased with the wide-ranging possibilities for evil of his plot: "Only to despite them I will endeavor anything" (31–32). It turns out that Hero is the one who is reputed to be killed by the calumniation, but all these imagined consequences seem to cheer Don John up: "Grow this to what adverse issue it can, I will put it in practice" (51–52). "Practice" is a familiar villain's word for a plot, and it is used frequently in this play. Benedick's suspicions immediately fall on Don John:

> The practice of it lives in John the bastard,
> Whose spirits toil in frame of villainies. (4.1.187–88)

Later Borachio confesses that Don John "paid me richly for the practice of it" (5.1.248–49).

Like most of Shakespeare's villains, Don John is an excellent actor. He seems energized by his plot, as if the vilifying of Hero and the breakup of her marriage is a sure cure for his depression. We see him reporting the bad news to Claudio and Don Pedro with a kind of glee. "The lady is disloyal.... Even she—Leonato's Hero, your Hero, every man's Hero" (3.2.100, 102–3). Don John is animated by his fictionalizing, as if he is only supplying the kind of "ocular proof" Othello demands of Iago (3.3.357). The word "disloyal"

> is too good to paint her wickedness. I could say she were worse. Think you
> of a worse title, and I will fit her to it. Wonder not till further warrant. Go
> but with me tonight, you shall see her chamber window ent'red, even the night
> before her wedding day. (105–10)

Don John is at his most triumphant here: "If you will follow me, I will show you enough; and when you have seen more and heard more, proceed accordingly" (116–18).

Once Hero has been rejected as a "rotten orange" (4.1.31), Don John disappears from the play. We learn in the next scene that he "is this morning secretly stol'n away" (4.2.61). After Borachio confesses to the plot, Don Pedro has a concluding judgment about his bastard brother: "He is composed and framed of treachery,/ And fled he is upon this villainy" (5.1.250–51). At the very end, Don Pedro learns that his "brother John is ta'en in flight,/ And brought with armèd men back to Messina" (5.4.125–26). Benedick concludes the play by declaring: "I'll devise thee brave punishments for him" (5.4.127–28), but nothing happens. The villainous Don John action is not developed sufficiently to serve as a counterbalance to the wit and charm of *Much Ado About Nothing*. Even Beatrice's imperious demand of Benedick: "Kill Claudio" (4.1.287) to prove his love has no real consequence in the play, which always remains a comedy with some tragicomic touches.

Iachimo in *Cymbeline* is a much more fully developed villain than Don John.[3] Emphasis is placed on his being a cunning Italian, a Machiavellian plotter. By his own admission, "mine Italian brain/ Gan in your duller Britain operate/ Most vilely" (196–98). Posthumus, now aware of the folly of the wager, calls him an "Italian fiend" (210):

> Egregious murderer, thief, anything
> That's due to all the villains past, in being,
> To come! (210–12)

Earlier, Pisanio, reading Posthumus's letter commanding him to murder Imogen, inveighs against italianate cunning:

> What false Italian,
> As poisonous-tongued as handed, hath prevailed
> On thy too ready hearing? (3.2.4–6)

Imogen blames the fatal letter on "drug-damned Italy," which has "outcraftied" her husband (3.4.14).

Finally, Sicilius, Posthumus's ghostly father, accuses Jupiter of letting matters go awry:

> Why did you suffer Iachimo, slight thing of Italy,
> To taint his [Posthumus's] nobler heart and brain with needless jealousy,
> And to become the geck [dupe] and scorn o' th' other's villainy? (5.4.47–49)

Iachimo's Italianate sophistication is like Iago's, whom he resembles not only in name, but also in the way he operates by stealth and trickery.

Iachimo's villainy already shows itself in the wager scene (I, iv). He vows that he can triumph over the chastity of any woman at all, so that the bet is not specifically about Imogen, but about Posthumus's blind faith in his wife's virtue. Iachimo boasts of his unlimited power over women:

> But I make my wager rather against your confidence than her reputation;
> and, to bar your offense herein too, I durst attempt it against any lady in
> the world. (116–19)

The credulous Posthumus, of course, doesn't realize that Iachimo will win his bet by any means, fair or foul. The wager is introduced by an account of last night's argument,

> where each of us fell in praise of our country mistresses; this gentleman
> [Posthumus] at that time vouching—and upon warrant of bloody
> affirmation—his to be more fair, virtuous, wise, chaste, constant, qualified, and
> less attemptable than any the rarest of our ladies in France. (60–65)

Iachimo immediately, and by an almost instinctive sense of manliness, asserts the negative: "That lady is not now living, or this gentleman's opinion, by this, worn out" (66–67). So the naïve Posthumus is drawn into the wager with Iachimo, who speaks with a kind of world-weary sophistication:

> you know strange fowl light upon neighboring ponds. Your ring may be
> stol'n too. So your brace of unprizable estimations, the one is but frail and the
> other casual. A cunning thief, or a that-way-accomplished courtier, would hazard
> the winning both of first and last. (93–99)

Iachimo, of course, is the cunning thief and the that-way-accomplished courtier. He seems to be trying to persuade Posthumus not to accept a bet he is certain to lose.

It is remarkable how confident Iachimo is in his ability to seduce any lady at all:

> With five times so much conversation I should get ground of your fair
> mistress, make her go back even to the yielding, had I admittance, and
> opportunity to friend. (109–12)

He is even willing to bet half of his estate to Posthumus's diamond ring, a bet that he considers wildly unequal, since his estate is presumably worth much more than a single diamond (a few lines further he sets a value of ten thousand ducats on half of his estate). As the scene progresses, Iachimo grows more contemptuous of his adversary:

> If you buy ladies' flesh at a million a dram, you cannot preserve it from tainting.
> But I see you have some religion in you, that you fear. (140–43)

Iachimo sounds very much like Iago in these lines, both in his cynicism about women, and in his scorn of religion. Iachimo and Iago are both confirmed atheists. The wager is drawn up as a legal contract, and Iachimo seems totally

unconcerned with the stipulation that if the lady "remains unseduced" (167) he
shall have to fight a duel with Posthumus. He is certain this will never happen.

By Act I, scene vi, Iachimo has arrived in Britain and is speaking with
Imogen. He seems to fall in love with her immediately—or at least to give
that impression. His aside expresses his concern, for the first time, that he
may lose the wager:

> Boldness be my friend!
> Arm me, audacity, from head to foot,
> Or like the Parthian I shall flying fight—
> Rather, directly fly. (18–21)

Notice how, like Tarquin in *The Rape of Lucrece*, Iachimo speaks of amorous
conflict in military terms. The Parthian archers (also mentioned in *Antony
and Cleopatra* III, i) were famous horsemen, who, while seeming to retreat,
shot their arrows backwards.

Iachimo has a variety of coherent plans for winning Imogen. The first is an
extravagant and euphuistical attack on Posthumus's indiscriminate lust in Italy:

> The cloyèd will—
> That satiate yet unsatisfied desire, that tub
> Both filled and running—ravening first the lamb,
> Longs after for the garbage. (47–50)

This echoes the Ghost's diatribe in *Hamlet* against both the Queen and
Claudius:

> So lust, though to a radiant angel linked,
> Will sate itself in a celestial bed
> And prey on garbage. (1.5.55–57)

Imogen doesn't understand Iachimo's rhetorical flights. In her astonishment,
she asks: "What is the matter, trow?" (47) and "What, dear sir,/ Thus raps
you? Are you well?" (50–51). This is the only occurrence of "raps" (meaning transports, carries you away) in Shakespeare. It is related to "rapt" in
Macbeth (1.3.57, 142).

Iachimo's next move is to offer himself to Imogen as a way of revenging
herself on Posthumus: "I dedicate myself to your sweet pleasure" (136). But
Imogen is angered by his obvious attempt at seduction:

If thou wert honorable,
Thou wouldst have told this tale for virtue, not
For such an end thou seek'st, as base as strange. (142–44)

At this point, when Imogen is calling for Pisanio and threatening to tell the King of Iachimo's "assault" (150), he suddenly switches to a different tack: it was all only a way of testing Imogen's chastity, which she has now proven beyond a doubt. The slippery Iachimo then launches into extravagant praise of Posthumus's virtue. When this is done, Iachimo then tries another tack. He will stow his trunk, full of rich gifts for the Emperor, in Imogen's bedchamber. She, too, like her husband, is trusting and credulous, to her great cost.

By the time we reach the highly erotic scene (II, ii) of Imogen asleep in her bed, we are ready for Iachimo's masterstroke. He emerges from the trunk to make a detailed "inventory" (30) of the room and of Imogen's body. He is meticulous in his endeavor: "I will write all down" (24). His long soliloquy here is eloquent and aesthetic, the most lyrical passage in the play. It is interesting that Iachimo compares himself to Tarquin, the ravisher in *The Rape of Lucrece*:

Our Tarquin thus
Did softly press the rushes ere he wakened
The chastity he wounded. (12–14)

It is clear that Iachimo understands this scene as a kind of rape.

He also alludes to the rape of Philomela in Ovid's *Metamorphoses*. Like Brutus turning down the leaf of his book before he goes to sleep—and right before the appearance of the Ghost of Caesar (*Julius Caesar* 4.3.272), Imogen also folds down the leaf of her Ovidean account of violent crime. Among his many detailed observations, Iachimo notes that Imogen has been reading "The tale of Tereus. Here the leaf's turned down/ Where Philomel gave up" (45–46). It is at this intensely literary moment that Iachimo says: "I have enough" (46) and reenters the trunk. In *Titus Andronicus* (IV, i) Lavinia also uses the Philomela story from the *Metamorphoses* to reveal that she was raped and mutilated.

In his description of Imogen's body, Iachimo speaks like a painter, and he goes well beyond what he needs to win the wager:

On her left breast
A mole cinque-spotted [with five spots], like the crimson drops
I' th' bottom of a cowslip. Here's a voucher
Stronger than ever law could make. This secret
Will force him think I have picked the lock and ta'en
The treasure of her honor. No more. (37–42)

It seems as if Iachimo is overwhelmed by the sweet excess of what he sees. Contrary to his villainous purposes, he seems to have fallen in love with Imogen's beauty.

When Iachimo returns to Italy and reports back to Poshumus, his narrative has developed many flourishes that are sure to present him as an invincible seducer, ironically, of course, since we know what has happened in Act II, scene ii. He boasts that Imogen was "so easy" (2.4.47). Iachimo luxuriates in aesthetic details about Imogen's bedchamber:

> the chimney-piece
> Chaste Dian bathing. Never saw I figures
> So likely to report [identify] themselves. The cutter [sculptor]
> Was as another Nature, dumb; outwent her,
> Motion and breath left out. (81–85)

This is like the Third Gentleman's report of Hermione's statue in *The Winter's Tale:*

> a piece many years in doing and now newly performed by that rare Italian master, Julio Romano, who, had he himself eternity and could put breath into his work, would beguile Nature of her custom, so perfectly he is her ape [imitator]. . . . (5.2.103–7)

In his artistic rapture, Iachimo is outdoing himself. He even invents dialogue for Imogen, who gave him her bracelet and said "She prized it once" (104), like Cressida giving Troilus's sleeve to Diomedes in *Troilus and Cressida* (V, ii). The narrative fulfills everything Posthumus needs to know from "This yellow Iachimo" (2.5.14). Yellow was a color associated with jealousy; it seems as if Posthumus is busy transferring his own jealousy to Iachimo. We remember that in *Twelfth Night* Malvolio wears very conspicuous "yellow stockings" (2.5.153) that are ridiculously inappropriate.

In Act V, scene ii, Posthumus, dressed *"like a poor soldier,"* subdues and disarms Iachimo, who is suitably contrite:

> The heaviness and guilt within my bosom
> Takes off my manhood. I have belied a lady,
> The princess of this country, and the air on't
> Revengingly enfeebles me. . . . (1–4)

At the end of the play, he confesses all: "By villainy/ I got this ring" (5.5.142–43). He then recounts in detail the scene of the wager (I, iv) and the scene in Imogen's bedchamber (II, ii):

my practice so prevailed
That I returned with similar [simulated] proof enough
To make the noble Leonatus mad
By wounding his belief in her renown
With tokens thus and thus. . . . (199–203)

Here again is the villain's word "practice," indicating a nefarious plot.

Iachimo is expansive in his confession, and just as he is warming to his peroration, Posthumus advances and cuts him off, calling him "Italian fiend" and upbraiding himself as

most credulous fool,
Egregious murderer, thief, anything
That's due to all the villains past, in being,
To come! (210–13)

He thinks that Imogen is dead and that he has killed her, but, of course, he is wrong and the disguised Imogen speaks at line 227. Now the numerous difficulties of the extremely complex plot are all explained away and the tragicomedy of *Cymbeline* ends happily.

The foul "practices" of Don John and Iachimo result in the supposed deaths of Hero and Imogen, but Lucio's slanders in *Measure for Measure* don't injure anyone. They only help to create a strongly negative and satirical tone in the play. His calumniations against the Duke have no immediate consequences, since they are mostly directed against the Duke in disguise as a friar. Nevertheless, they contribute to the darker tone of the play as a tragicomedy. Another way of looking at Lucio's calumniations is that they suggest certain harsh, satirical truths about the Duke that we need in order to understand what *Measure for Measure* is really about. This would place Lucio among a group of Shakespeare's unpleasant satirical commentators like Thersites in *Troilus and Cressida*, Apemantus in *Timon of Athens*, and Jaques in *As You Like It*, who are all, nevertheless, truth speakers.

In Act III, scene ii, Lucio refuses bail to keep Pompey, Mistress Overdone's servant, from going to prison. He jests about Pompey's function as a bawd or pimp and cruelly denies him any kind words or compassion:

I will pray, Pompey, to increase your bondage. If you take it not patiently, why, your mettle [spirit] is the more. Adieu, trusty Pompey. (75–77)

This leads directly to Lucio's conversation with the disguised Duke:

It was a mad fantastical trick of him to steal from the state, and usurp
the beggary he was never born to. Lord Angelo dukes it well in his absence;
he puts transgression to't. (94–97)

Lucio means to contrast Angelo's severity toward lechery with the Duke's lenity—if not his actual fondness for fornication. Lucio echoes Apemantus's rebuke of Timon: "Thou'dst courtier be again/ Wert thou not beggar" (*Timon of Athens* 4.3.242–43). The Duke tries in vain to disagree with Lucio, but he does not want to go so far as to reveal himself.

Lucio tirelessly contrasts the icy Angelo with the warm-spirited Duke:

Ere he would have hanged a man for the getting a hundred bastards, he would
have paid for the nursing of a thousand. He had some feeling of the sport; he
knew the service, and that instructed him to mercy. (119–23)

Lucio endows the Duke with strong sexual impulses, which the Duke vigorously denies: "I never heard the absent Duke much detected for women; he was not inclined that way" (124–25). This does not mean that the Duke was homosexual—only continent in his desires—but there is no stopping the slanderous Lucio. He accuses the Duke of having to do with

your beggar of fifty, and his use was to put a ducat in her clack-dish;
the Duke had crotchets [eccentricities] in him. He would be drunk too;
that let me inform you. (128–31)

Is Lucio speaking ironically in praise of the Duke or is he calumniating him? The Duke, growing more angry, is sure that Lucio is slandering him.

He certainly is when he leads the Duke on by saying "the greater file of the subject held the Duke to be wise," to which the Duke, taking the bait, replies: "Wise! Why, no question but he was." Lucio then springs his surprising conclusion: "A very superficial, ignorant, unweighing fellow" (139–42). There is no ambiguity about this slanderous remark, which the Duke, despite his great effort, is powerless to contradict. In Lucio's final speech in this scene, he continues to attribute to the absent Duke a rampant and random sexuality. He

would eat mutton on Fridays. He's not past it, yet, and I say to thee, he
would mouth with a beggar, though she smelled brown bread and garlic.
(182–85)

Friday was supposed to be a fast day, when meat was forbidden, but "mutton" is also a slang word for a prostitute.

After Lucio exits, the Duke concludes with a moral observation about the nature of calumny:

No might nor greatness in mortality
Can censure 'scape; back-wounding calumny
The whitest virtue strikes. What king so strong
Can tie the gall up in the slanderous tongue? (187–90)

This is one among many of the Duke's gnomic reflections on abstract ethical issues, a type of discourse characteristic of this play.

Lucio is remarkably consistent. As he says to the Duke at the end of Act IV, scene iii, "If bawdy talk offend you, we'll have very little of it. Nay, friar, I am a kind of burr; I shall stick" (180–81). This is proverbial (Tilley B724). In his own roundabout way, Lucio always thinks of the Duke as warm-hearted, as we see when he tries to comfort Isabella on the supposed death of her brother: "If the old fantastical Duke of dark corners had been at home, he had lived" (159–60). Lucio is thoroughly scabrous in his slanders against the Duke: "he's a better woodman than thou tak'st him for" (164–65), a woodman being a hunter of women. He confesses that he once came before the Duke "for getting a wench with child" (171–72), but he forswore it: "they would else have married me to the rotten medlar" (175–76). A "medlar" was a fruit, like a persimmon, eaten only when very ripe or partially rotten. It has strong sexual connotations and often referred to a prostitute. In Mercutio's bawdy discourse in *Romeo and Juliet*, love

will sit under a medlar tree
And wish his mistress were that kind of fruit
As maids call medlars when they laugh alone. (2.1.34–36)

By the end of the play, when everyone expects the Duke to mete out punishments, he remembers this wench whom Lucio has impregnated.

Lucio persists in his calumniations right up to the moment when the Duke is unmasked. The point of Act V, scene i seems to be that it is impossible for Lucio to be silent. He wants to have a commanding role in all the revelations at the denouement of the play. Lucio declares the disguised Duke to be

a meddling friar,
I do not like the man. Had he been lay, my lord,
For certain words he spake against your Grace
In your retirement, I had swinged [beaten] him soundly. (127–30)

Lucio is irrepressible in his fantasy, always busy inventing scenes and dialogue. It is "a saucy friar,/ A very scurvy [loathsome] fellow" (135–36). Later
he says that the friar is "honest in nothing but his clothes, and one that hath
spoke most villainous speeches of the Duke" (263–65). Lucio seems to be
wound up to speak nothing but slander against the friar:

> Why, you bald-pated, lying rascal, you must be hooded, must you? Show
> your knave's visage, with a pox to you. Show your sheep-biting face, and be
> hanged an hour. (354–57)

"Sheep-biting" is a strong word for a dog or wolf that attacked sheep,
hence a rogue, especially a hypocritical one like a Puritan. It is at this
point that Lucio *"Pulls off the friar's hood, and discovers the Duke"*
(358 s.d.).

It is significant that Lucio is the one person whom the Duke has diffi-
culty in pardoning. He doesn't deal with him until everyone else has been
judged:

> You, sirrah, that knew me for a fool, a coward,
> One all of luxury [lasciviousness], an ass, a madman;
> Wherein have I so deserved of you,
> That you extol me thus? (503–6)

The Duke seems genuinely hurt and puzzled by Lucio's calumny, but Lucio
only offers a casual and superficial explanation:

> Faith, my lord, I spoke it but according to the trick. If you will hang me for
> it, you may; but I had rather it would please you I might be whipped. (507–9)

"Trick" means something like fashion, custom, ordinary usage. Lucio is
no self-conscious, guilty penitent like Angelo. He wants the Duke to be
assured that there was no personal animus in his calumniations. The Duke
punishes him by making him marry the whore he has gotten with child.
Lucio's final line in the play is a protest against what he considers his
draconian fate: "Marrying a punk, my lord, is pressing to death, whipping,
and hanging" (525–26). He is certain that the Duke has dealt more harshly
with him than with anyone else in the play, especially Angelo, who is a
real villain.

All of the calumniators we have discussed are characters in comedies. By
the nature of the comic genre, their possibilities of evil-doing are limited,
and we know that everything will turn out well in the happy ending. That
is why the calumniators as a group are different from the villains in Shakespeare's tragedies and history plays. They may make dire threats, but these
tend to come to nothing. In the comedies in general there are many blocking

characters who contribute to the perturbations of the comic action. The difficulties they raise are always resolved by the end of the play.

NOTES

1. See Coleridge's *Shakespearean Criticism*, 2 vols., ed. Thomas Middleton Raysor, I, 44.

2. See Claire McEachern's Arden edition of *Much Ado*, London, 2006, pp. 17–19. McEachern emphasizes Don John's bastardy.

3. See A. A. Stephenson, "The Significance of *Cymbeline*," *Scrutiny*, 10 (1942), 329–38. This essay is an answer to an earlier piece in *Scrutiny* by F. C. Tinkler, 7 (1938), 5–20. See also the comments on Iachimo in Bertrand Evans, *Shakespeare's Comedies*, London, UK: Oxford University Press, 1960, pp. 245–89. Evans calls Iachimo "the smoothest of Shakespeare's villains" (p. 255).

Chapter 11

Tyrants:

Julius Caesar, Leontes, and Duke Frederick

I would like to speak about Shakespeare's tyrants in this chapter. Of course, there are a great many more tyrants than we can consider here—for example, Antiochus in *Pericles* and Creon in *The Two Noble Kinsmen*. Some, like Richard III and Macbeth, who are both also villains, we have already talked about. Julius Caesar is not directly a villain, since he is not involved in anyone's murder, but he speaks in the haughty language of villains, and his death brings about a bloody civil war in Rome. Julius Caesar resembles the villains of the tragedies and history plays because of his insistence on his autocratic will to the exclusion of any personal or compassionate motives. Leontes and Duke Frederick are tyrants in comedies, which limit the scope of their villainy, although Leontes's mad jealousy of his wife Hermione leads to the deaths of his son Mamillius and his court counselor Antigonus, and to the supposed deaths of Hermione and her daughter Perdita. We can see the workings of *The Winter's Tale* as a tragicomedy. In *As You Like It* Duke Frederick, the usurper, banishes Rosalind, the daughter of Duke Senior, who takes with her into exile Frederick's own daughter, Celia. What happens with the Duke is paralleled by the relation of Orlando to his older brother, Oliver, who plots his death.

Julius Caesar echoes *Richard III* in the devious and staged way in which Richard, Duke of Gloucester, with the help of Buckingham, "reluctantly" accepts the kingship (III, vii). Caesar, of course, never becomes king, but Casca's report of what happens in the market place (I, ii) suggests a similar kind of political manipulation:

I saw Mark Antony offer him a crown—yet 'twas not a crown neither, 'twas one of these coronets—and, as I told you, he put it by once; but for all that, to my thinking, he would fain have had it. Then he offered it to him again; then he put it by again; but to my thinking, he was very loath to lay his fingers off it. (235–41)

Casca is represented as "a blunt fellow" (295), not at all subtle, but the scene he describes so satirically is pure theater.

As in *Richard III*, there are three separate attempts to crown Caesar. Casca continues:

And then he offered it the third time. He put it the third time by; and still as he refused it, the rabblement hooted, and clapped their chopt [chapped] hands, and threw up their sweaty nightcaps, and uttered such a deal of stinking breath because Caesar refused the crown, that it had, almost, choked Caesar; for he swounded and fell down at it. (241–48)

Among many physical infirmities, Caesar (like Othello) has the falling sickness, or epilepsy, which ends his attempted coronation by Antony: "He fell down in the market place, and foamed at mouth, and was speechless" (253–54).

Casca understands that, except for the falling-sickness, it is all histrionic and an empty show:

If the tag-rag people did not clap him and hiss him, according as he pleased
and displeased them, as they use to do the players in the theater, I am no
true man. (258–61)

Richard and Julius Caesar both have contempt for the people, although their hypocritical affection has no curb. This is a forecast of issues that will be central to *Coriolanus*.

Julius Caesar is loaded with portents that give the play, like *Macbeth*, a sense of cosmic importance. Also, great attention is paid to Caesar's physical infirmities. Neither of these two enhancements of the tragic effect are needed in *Richard III*, but they are extremely important to Cassius. He goes to great length to describe several occasions on which the mighty Caesar proved himself to be a mere mortal. Cassius is passionate in his attempt to win Brutus to the conspiracy:

I had as lief not be, as live to be
In awe of such a thing as I myself.
I was born free as Caesar; so were you:
We both have fed as well, and we can both
Endure the winter's cold as well as he. . . . (95–99)

This kind of argument seems supremely irrelevant in a political discussion. What difference could it make that Brutus and Cassius have "fed as well" as Caesar, or that they can, like Caesar, "Endure the winter's cold'? Yet Brutus listens to Cassius intently and is eventually persuaded to join the conspiracy.

Cassius's account of the swimming match with Caesar in the Tiber hardly seems to have any political content, but to Cassius it is supremely important as a way of demonstrating his own superior manliness:

> For once, upon a raw and gusty day,
> The troubled Tiber chafing with her shores,
> Caesar said to me "Dar'st thou, Cassius, now
> Leap in with me into this angry flood,
> And swim to yonder point?" Upon the word,
> Accout'red as I was, I plungèd in
> And bade him follow: so indeed he did.
> The torrent roared, and we did buffet it
> With lusty sinews, throwing it aside
> And stemming it with hearts of controversy. (100–9)

Cassius recounts this story to Brutus with verve and panache, particularly the part that shows how much stronger he is than the effeminate Caesar:

> But ere we could arrive the point proposed,
> Caesar cried "Help me, Cassius, or I sink!"
> I, as Aeneas, our great ancestor,
> Did from the flames of Troy upon his shoulder
> The old Anchises bear, so from the waves of Tiber
> Did I the tired Caesar. And this man
> Is now become a god, and Cassius is
> A wretched creature, and must bend his body
> If Caesar carelessly but nod on him. (110–18)

So, alluding to the *Aeneid*, Cassius becomes the heroic warrior Aeneas who rescued his aged father Anchises (imaged now as the once-mighty Caesar) from the ruins of Troy.

Cassius's next narrative is even more demeaning to Caesar:

> He had a fever when he was in Spain,
> And when the fit was on him, I did mark
> How he did shake; 'tis true, this god did shake.
> His coward lips did from their color fly,
> And that same eye whose bend doth awe the world
> Did lose his luster; I did hear him groan;
> Ay, and that tongue of his, that bade the Romans
> Mark him and write his speeches in their books,
> Alas, it cried, "Give me some drink, Titinius,"

As a sick girl. Ye gods! It doth amaze me,
A man of such a feeble temper should
So get the start of the majestic world,
And bear the palm alone. (119–31)

So what bearing could Caesar's "feeble temper," or weak constitution, have on the political fate of Rome? All the while Cassius and Brutus are speaking, they hear shouts from the market place "For some new honors that are heaped on Caesar" (134). Brutus strives to be a rational man, but he is certainly moved by what Cassius recounts and by the shouts of the Roman populace.

In no other play of Shakespeare, except perhaps *Richard III*, is the tyrant (or villain) endowed with so many physical infirmities as Caesar is. This sets up a sharp contrast between Caesar the man and Caesar the great Roman warrior who wants to be king (or emperor). Shakespeare goes out of his way to add details that hardly seem to be necessary; for example, when Caesar is speaking to Antony about Cassius, we are startled by a new revelation:

I rather tell thee what is to be feared
Than what I fear; for always I am Caesar.
Come on my right hand, for this ear is deaf,
And tell me truly what thou think'st of him. (211–14)

Shakespeare invents this detail of Caesar's being deaf in his left ear. In context, there seems to be a dramatic contrast between Caesar's rhetorical bluster—"for always I am Caesar"—and his glaring physical inadequacies.

Like Iago (as in *Othello* I, iii) or Edmund (as in *King Lear* I, ii), Julius Caesar is a creature of strong and determined personal will, a significant mark of the tyrant. Act II, scene ii is a domestic scene with Caesar entering in his "nightgown," or dressing gown. Calphurnia, his wife, has dreamt of his murder, and she insists "You shall not stir out of your house today" (9). But Caesar is insistent and he speaks of himself in an oddly impersonal way (always in the third person):

Caesar shall forth. The things that threatened me
Ne'er looked but on my back; when they shall see
The face of Caesar, they are vanishèd. (10–12)

This seems to validate Cassius's argument that the man Caesar, whom all Romans adore, has merged with Caesar as a political institution, with its threat of tyranny. Calphurnia offers a strong argument, amplified by frightening portents, for her husband's need to stay at home.

But Caesar remains unpersuaded, and he speaks again in fatalistic, Stoic terms:

What can be avoided
Whose end is purposed by the mighty gods?
Yet Caesar shall go forth; for these predictions
Are to the world in general as to Caesar. (26–29)

In other words, Calphurnia's dreams have no personal validity.

Throughout this scene, Caesar speaks with a kind of oratorical bluster or rant. He utterly rejects what his augurers have told him:

Caesar should be a beast without a heart
If he should stay at home today for fear.
No, Caesar shall not; Danger knows full well
That Caesar is more dangerous than he.
We are two lions littered in one day,
And I the older and more terrible,
And Caesar shall go forth. (42–48)

He enters so wholeheartedly into the personification with Danger that it seems as if he objectifies himself as a system of personifications rather than as a fallible human being. When he finally decides to take Calphurnia's advice and stay at home, Decius, a Roman conspirator, appears to accompany him to the Senate House.

We know from the previous scene that Decius is confident that he can deliver Caesar to the Capitol because he is so easily subject to flattery. Decius boasts: "For I can give his humor the true bent" (2.1.210). Caesar's immediate reaction to Decius is to assert his imperial prerogatives:

Tell them that I will not come today.
Cannot, is false; and that I dare not, falser:
I will not come today. (2.2.62–64)

The emphasis here is on Caesar's implacable and incontrovertible will, as he declares flatly: "The cause is in my will: I will not come" (71). But this feeds easily into Decius's flattering reinterpretation of Calphurnia's dream, followed by his assertion: "the Senate have concluded/ To give this day a crown to mighty Caesar" (94). There is no way Caesar can resist this temptation, which has no basis in fact. He makes the fatal decision to go to the Senate, along with the many bustling conspirators who intend to murder him.

Caesar is at his most imperious in the scene of his assassination (III, i). It is here, in the assertion of his unchallengeable will, that he closely resembles Shakespeare's villains. He speaks in a grandiose style, as if he already were the Emperor of Rome. For example, when Artemidorus presents a petition, presumably to warn him about the conspiracy, Caesar answers magisterially: "What touches us ourself shall be last served" (8). The conspirators have planned their strategy well, beginning with Metellus Cimber's plea for his banished brother. Caesar's answer is so extravagant in rejecting any human fallibility in himself that we are astounded by his effrontery:

> Be not fond
> To think that Caesar bears such rebel blood
> That will be thawed from the true quality
> With that which melteth fools—I mean sweet words,
> Low-crookèd curtsies, and base spaniel fawning. (39–43)

Caesar's provocative vaunting endows the assassination with a powerful and immediate cause.

Caesar's long speech to Metellus Cimber ends with gross and injurious insults:

> Thy brother by decree is banishèd.
> If thou dost bend and pray and fawn for him,
> I spurn thee like a cur out of my way.
> Know, Caesar doth not wrong, nor without cause
> Will he be satisfied. (44–48)

Ben Jonson in *Timber* thought the last two lines were ridiculous,[1] but there is an inflation of rhetoric throughout this speech. Shylock, too, confronts Antonio with a similar dog image:

> You that did void your rheum upon my beard
> And foot me as you spurn a stranger cur
> Over your threshold! (*The Merchant of Venice* 1.3.114–16)

This is an insult Antonio repeats a few lines further.

Caesar's claim to a god-like impassivity grows stronger as he humiliates Metellus Cimber. Caesar is not a man like other men, subject to emotional influences:

> I could be well moved, if I were as you;
> If I could pray to move, prayers would move me;

But I am constant as the Northern Star,
Of whose true-fixed and resting [changeless] quality
There is no fellow in the firmament. (58–62)

He luxuriates in images of his will as being of star-like constancy, and it is at this point that the conspirators stab him.

Like Caesar, Leontes in *The Winter's Tale* plays the tyrant in his mad rage over what he supposes is the infidelity of his pregnant wife, Hermione. Here, too, there is a close stylistic link between tyrant and villain. Leontes is directly responsible for the deaths of his son Mamillius and his counselor Antigonus, and also, he thinks, for the deaths of Hermione and his daughter. So his paranoid rage has grave consequences. Once he slips into jealousy, Leontes speaks with a passionate energy, especially evident in his feverish repetition of words. As he exclaims in an aside:

Too hot, too hot!
To mingle friendship far is mingling bloods.
I have tremor cordis [palpitations of the heart] on me; my heart dances,
But not for joy, not joy. (1.2.108–11)

Leontes's fit comes upon him suddenly, without any transition or build up. He sees evidences of adultery that are invisible to the audience:

But to be paddling palms and pinching fingers,
As now they are, and making practiced smiles
As in a looking glass; and then to sigh, as 'twere
The mort [death] o' th' deer—oh, that is entertainment
My bosom likes not, nor my brows. (115–18)

This is like the closet scene in *Hamlet* (III, iv), where Hamlet attributes a hot and heavy lustfulness to Claudius and his mother that we never actually witness:

Let the bloat King tempt you again to bed,
Pinch wanton on your cheek, call you his mouse,
And let him, for a pair of reechy [smoky, filthy] kisses
Or paddling in your neck with his damned fingers,
Make you to ravel all this matter out. . . . (183–87)

Tyranny and villainy are closely allied as Leontes moves immediately to have his chief counselor, Camillo, poison his best friend, Polixenes. Again, Leontes is inflamed with grossly sexual signs of his wife's affair with his friend:

Is whispering nothing?
Is leaning cheek to cheek? Is meeting noses?
Kissing with inside lip? Stopping the career
Of laughter with a sigh (a note infallible
Of breaking honesty)? Horsing foot on foot?
Skulking in corners? (284–89)

It's obvious that Leontes can't possibly see all that he is describing—for example, "Kissing with inside lip"—but as he imagines these lascivious acts, he becomes wilder in his jealousy. He reviles the good Camillo for defending Hermione:

I say thou liest, Camillo, and I hate thee,
Pronounce thee a gross lout, a mindless slave,
Or else a hovering temporizer, that
Canst with thine eyes at once see good and evil,
Inclining to them both. (300–4)

Camillo informs Polixenes that Leontes wants to murder him, and they both flee.

As Leontes's jealousy becomes more uncontrollable, he asserts his naked will as opposed to all rationality and good counsel. By Act II, scene i he is speaking like Iago or Richard, Duke of Glooucester. He doesn't need anyone else's opinion, as he angrily exclaims:

Why, what need we
Commune with you of this, but rather follow
Our forceful instigation? Our prerogative
Calls not your counsels, but our natural goodness
Imparts this; which, if you, or stupefied,
Or seeming so, in skill [reason], cannot, or will not,
Relish a truth like us, inform yourselves,
We need no more of your advice. (161–68)

Notice how breathless and broken the syntax is and also how Leontes, like Caesar, refers to himself with the imperial "we."

There is a strong emphasis on Leontes's tyranny in Act II, scene iii, and Act III, scene ii, with the word and its correlates repeated at least ten times. Paulina speaks of Leontes's "tyrannous passion" (2.3.27) and develops the idea in direct confrontation with the King:

I'll not call you tyrant;
But this most cruel usage of your queen

(Not able to produce more accusation
Than your own weak-hinged fancy) something savors
Of tyranny, and will ignoble make you,
Yea, scandalous to the world. (114–19)

But Leontes is impervious to any persuasion, as we can tell from his illogical argument: "Were I a tyrant,/ Where were her life?" (120–21). Hermione's trial in Act III, scene ii, of course, is directed at her life, which, along with the actual death of her son Mamillius, she seems to lose.

In the trial scene Leontes goes through the motions of justice in order to avoid the accusation of tyranny. At the very beginning, he declares:

Let us be cleared
Of being tyrannous, since we so openly
Proceed in justice, which shall have due course,
Even to the guilt or the purgation. (4–7)

This is a show trial, like that of Queen Katherine in *Henry VIII*. Hermione pleads eloquently in her defense:

if powers divine
Behold our human actions—as they do—
I doubt not then, but Innocence shall make
False Accusation blush, and Tyranny
Tremble at Patience. (27–31)

But there is no way of reaching Leontes, even through the timid medium of personification.

The oracle from Delphos cannot convince the King:

"Hermione is chaste, Polixenes blameless, Camillo a true subject, Leontes a jealous tyrant, his innocent babe truly begotten. . . ." (130–33)

It is only with the death of his son Mamillius that Leontes realizes "Apollo's angry, and the heavens themselves/ Do strike at my injustice" (143–44). But then Hermione faints and Paulina pronounces her dead: "This news is mortal to the Queen" (145). Does Paulina already have a long-range plan to wait sixteen years while the penitent Leontes grieves, then bring Hermione back to life? Paulina drives home the point of the disastrous effects of Leontes's tyranny. She holds, as it were, his feet to the fire:

What studied torments, tyrant, hast for me? . . .
Thy tyranny,

Together working with thy jealousies,
Fancies too weak for boys, too green and idle
For girls of nine—O, think what they have done,
And then run mad indeed, stark mad. . . . (173, 177–81)

From this moment on, she becomes Leontes's spiritual counselor and nurtures his penitence and eventual revivification.

But she is merciless in her attack on the King:

But, O thou tyrant,
Do not repent these things, for they are heavier
Than all thy woes can stir; therefore betake thee
To nothing but despair. (205–8)

Despair is a serious spiritual condition, indicating a lack of belief in God's providence. It usually leads to suicide, but *The Winter's Tale* asserts its healing, tragicomic perspective by producing, after sixteen years, a thoroughly happy ending, in which Hermione comes alive and is joyously reunited with her husband; her daughter Perdita reappears and is married to Florizel, the son of Polixenes; and, to cap it all off, Paulina is wed to Camillo.

Some of the same ideas about the irrationality, capriciousness, and harmful effects of tyranny are also seen in Duke Frederick in *As You Like It*. He is a usurper of the kingdom of his brother, Duke Senior, who now lives, like Robin Hood and his Merry Men, in idyllic exile in the Forest of Arden. When Orlando, the youngest son of Sir Rowland de Boys, wins the match against the Duke's wrestler, Duke Frederick is displeased:

I would thou hadst been son to some man else.
The world esteemed thy father honorable,
But I did find him still mine enemy. (1.2.214–16)

Celia apologizes for her father's "rough and envious disposition" (231), but we never discover the cause of the Duke's displeasure. He is "humorous" (256), or capricious, and Orlando is banished from the kingdom.

He ends the scene with a resigned couplet:

Thus must I from the smoke into the smother [smothering smoke],
From tyrant Duke unto a tyrant brother. (277–78)

Rosalind, Duke Senior's daughter, must leave too, but Celia, Duke Frederick's daughter, insists on accompanying her to the Forest of Arden. Like all tyrants in Shakespeare, the Duke does not deign to offer any explanation: "Thou art thy father's daughter, there's enough" (1.3.56), and "Firm and irrevocable is my doom" (81).

Orlando's older brother, Oliver, appears in the first scene of the play, and there is an ingenious twinning of Oliver and Duke Frederick as tyrants. Oliver has neglected to bring up his younger brother, Orlando, as a gentleman, according to the will of his father. Orlando protests his debasement:

> Shall I keep your hogs and eat husks with them? What prodigal portion
> have I spent that I should come to such penury? (1.1.36–38)

Oliver strikes him and Orlando fights back, threatening his brother with injury. Speaking always with haughty disdain, Oliver asserts his superiority: "Wilt thou lay hands upon me, villain" (54)? "Villain" was a standard term for a serf or bondman, but there is also wordplay on "villain" as an evildoer. Orlando refuses to accept the demeaning term:

> I am no villain. I am the youngest son of Sir Rowland de Boys; he was my
> father, and he is thrice a villain that says such a father begot villains. (55–57)

But Oliver has a plan about how to get rid of his troublesome brother. In his conversation with the Duke's wrestler, Charles, Oliver slanders Orlando:

> I assure thee, and almost with tears I speak it, there is not one so young and
> so villainous this day living. I speak but brotherly of him. . . . (147–49)

So the wrestler is entreated, like a paid assassin, to get rid of him. Oliver's final soliloquy shows him as a committed villain who will stop at nothing: "I hope I shall see an end of him; for my soul, yet I know not why, hates nothing more than he" (157–59).

Oliver and Duke Frederick, both tyrants, come together in Act III, scene i. The Duke has dispatched Oliver to find his brother Orlando on pain of banishment and forfeiture. Oliver's protests are, of course, completely misdirected:

> O that your Highness knew my heart in this!
> I never loved my brother in my life. (13–14)

Even the hard-hearted Duke is scandalized:

> More villain thou. Well, push him out of doors,
> And let my officers of such a nature
> Make an extent upon his house and lands. (15–17)

None of these dire predictions have any consequence, since Oliver is mysteriously redeemed and becomes the lover of Celia, and the Duke is also converted to a religious life. The tyranny of Oliver and the Duke is thus neutralized by the unpredictable comic action. Tyrants are not necessarily villains, although they share many characteristics, especially an indomitable will that separates them from their fellow human beings. They are ruthlessly self-determined. Julius Caesar is almost a caricature of an overweening creature of will. His lofty insistence on his not-to-be-questioned power easily plays into the hands of the conspirators and leads to his murder. Leontes and Duke Frederick, both tyrants in comedy, are quite different from Julius Caesar. We already anticipate the happy ending in comedy, so we are sure that neither Leontes nor Duke Frederick can continue in their tyrannical behavior. Comedy as a genre needs the perturbations provided by tyrants and other blocking characters, but we know that they cannot prevail.

NOTE

1. See the Arden edition of *Julius Caesar*, ed. David Daniell, London, 1998, pp. 136–37.

Conclusion

Iago is Shakespeare's archetypal villain. The despairing Othello asks Cassio at the very end of the play: "Will you, I pray, demand that devil [Iago]/ Why he hath thus ensnared my soul and body?" In his final speech, Iago says only: "Demand me nothing. What you know, you know./ From this time forth I never will speak word" (5.2.297–300). So Othello is left unsatisfied and Iago ends as a total, diabolic villain. Don John, too, in *Much Ado About Nothing*, is curiously like Iago in not offering any explanations for his villainy. This makes him seem detached from his play.

There usually is some attempt, often truncated, at reformation for the villains at the end of their plays. Edmund in *King Lear*, for example, suddenly remembers that he has ordered the deaths of Lear and Cordelia in prison. When he is defeated by Edgar in single combat, he abruptly tries to undo his writ:

I pant for life. Some good I mean to do,
Despite of mine own nature. Quickly send—
Be brief in it—to the castle, for my writ
Is on the life of Lear and on Cordelia;
Nay, send in time. (5.3.241–45)

Lear is still alive, but Cordelia is probably already dead.

Shakespeare makes an important effort to modify our sense that his villains are totally depraved. In *Titus Andronicus*, for example, the heartless Moor Aaron is seen at the end to be in love with his black baby. Before his gruesome and gleeful recital of his evil deeds, he demands assurance from Lucius that he will save his child "And bear it from me to the Empress" (5.1.54). His paternal solicitude doesn't fit with his fiendlike catalogue of all the evils he has done or plans to do, but he makes Lucius swear that his child will be spared. So Aaron's villainy seems mitigated.

The villain's feeling of guilt also plays an important role in making him seem sympathetic. The asides of Claudius in *Hamlet* and his long soliloquy in Act III, scene iii make us aware that he is acutely conscious of his own evil-doing. He knows that his

> offence is rank, it smells to heaven;
> It hath the primal eldest curse upon't,
> A brother's murder. (36–38)

Claudius makes no effort to lessen his offence—it stinks (the basic meaning of "rank"). He also makes an important distinction between what one can get away with in this world, but not in the judgment of heaven: "There is no shuffling" (61). In terms of guilt, for example, Tarquin's rape of Lucrece is so emphatically punished by his own conscience that we are almost persuaded that he acts beyond the control of his own conscious will.

These issues are most powerfully developed in *Macbeth*. Macbeth is unusual among Shakespeare's villains in being a villain-hero, so that he seems almost from the beginning of the play to be rescued from utter moral obliquity. He offers such compelling reasons for not committing the murders that we almost believe that he will not do them. But of course he does. It is interesting in this play how much Macbeth suffers physically, especially from insomnia. Sleep becomes a magical peaceful state associated with innocence:

> Sleep that knits up the raveled sleave of care,
> The death of each day's life, sore labor's bath,
> Balm of hurt minds, great nature's second course,
> Chief nourisher in life's feast. . . . (2.2.36–39)

Macbeth ends in a state of spiritual desiccation and despair, and Lady Macbeth goes mad with haunting dreams of blood and guilt.

In *Richard III* the King's conscience bothers him at the end of the play, when the ghosts of all the persons he has murdered appear to haunt him before the battle of Bosworth Field. Richard suddenly starts up out of his dream:

> Have mercy, Jesu! Soft! I did but dream.
> O coward conscience, how dost thou afflict me! (5.3.179–80)

He is self-judged as a villain:

> My conscience hath a thousand several tongues,
> And every tongue brings in a several tale,
> And every tale condemns me for a villain. (194–96)

This powerful emotional speech ends in a frightening conclusion:

> I shall despair. There is no creature loves me;
> And if I die, no soul will pity me. (201–2)

Richard is close to Macbeth at this point.

In *The Merchant of Venice,* Shylock's villainy is balanced against Antonio's overt anti-Semitism and the crassness of a slave-holding Venetian society. We should also include Jessica's abandonment of her father and her stealing of his jewels and money, along with Portia's tricky "quality of mercy" speech by which Shylock is diminished both financially and spiritually. There is no doubt that Shylock is a villain, but his intense speech about the essential humanity of Jews is memorable as a kind of counterstatement:

> Hath not a Jew eyes? Hath not a Jew hands, organs, dimensions, senses, affections, passions?—fed with the same food, hurt with the same weapons, subject to the same diseases, healed by the same means, warmed and cooled by the same winter and summer as a Christian is? (3.1.55–61)

These are questions that cannot comfortably be answered in the society of Venice.

In Shakespeare's comedies, these redemptive motives in the creation of villains are not so strongly in evidence as in the tragedies. *Measure for Measure* is a tragicomedy, an in-between genre, but Angelo is pardoned at the end by the Duke, by Mariana, and by Isabella. This occurs despite the fact that he has been tested and found wanting by the Duke almost from the beginning of the play. Angelo definitely thinks that Claudio has been put to death, despite his unsavory bargain with Claudio's sister, Isabella. *Romeo and Juliet* is technically a tragedy, but it begins like a comedy, in which Tybalt, the Italianate swordsman, seems an entirely inappropriate figure. He is a very histrionic character, who represents the persistence of a mysterious feud everyone seems to want to forget about. He murders Mercutio while he is being protected under Romeo's arm. But once Tybalt has been killed by Romeo, he generates a great deal of sympathetic grief from the Capulets, including the newly-married Juliet. It is significant how much Shakespeare softens his villains and gives them redeeming qualities, including an active conscience, or else puts them in a context of a corrupt society.

In this sense, the villains have an important creative link with the author,[1] who is also plotting industriously (and, of course, is the ultimate source of the villains' plotting). We tend to think of Iago, for example, as inventive in his own right. He clearly takes over the play from Othello, at least in terms of what fascinates audiences. In this way the villains seem very close to

Shakespeare himself and to the hidden secrets of his imagination. The study of imagery has been used to show Shakespeare's preoccupations in his plays. In *Hamlet*, for example, we discover the odd prominence of images of skin disease, images of inner and secret skin disease like the "imposthume," "That inward breaks, and shows no cause without/ Why the man dies" (4.4.27–29).[2] Shakespeare no doubt had some uncanny feeling for evil—not just mischief, but real, diabolical evil—that we would love to understand more comprehensively than we now do. We reject as simple-minded the notion of using Shakespeare's characters as a guide to understanding the author's psyche, a common practice in the Shakespeare criticism of the nineteenth century, an approach to Shakespeare's biography that is still with us.

After this long and detailed study of Shakespeare's villains (and calumniators and tyrants), what can we conclude about Shakespeare's imaginative world? One obvious point is that despite his joyous comedies, Shakespeare presents a dark view of reality. His villains are so clever and so powerful, as if the virtuous characters in the tragedies and history plays don't stand a chance against the villains. The virtuous characters, by their very honesty, seem so naïve and easily duped. Aristotle's *Poetics* reminds us that the fate of the tragic characters could very well be ours. We feel so strongly for them because they are like us or at least because we share in the tragic protagonists' strong feelings. As human beings, we fear that we all can suffer the same tragic fate. It's worth remembering how imaginative and inventive the villains seem, how brilliant at improvisation. These are qualities that we all admire. The villains are also generally excellent speakers, very persuasive, and amazing in their ability to play a wide variety of different roles.

It is interesting that what is best remembered as Shakespeare's contribution to other Elizabethan and Jacobean dramatists is his creation of villains. The dramatists who seem most Shakespearean, like Middleton and Webster, are notable for their creations of memorable villains in the Shakespearean mode. Middleton's De Flores in *The Changeling* (1622) is brilliant in his perceptions about the consequences of murder; he brings the flighty Beatrice-Joanna to a bitter sense of the reality in which she now exists. Middleton's Livia in *Women Beware Women* (1621), an extremely intricate play, has a masterful understanding of human psychology, and she can fashion other characters according to her iron will.

Webster is the dramatist who is most often said to be Shakespearean, and I think it is because of Webster's skill in developing a tragic sense. This comes to a large extent from his brilliant villains, who are murderous and meditative at the same time. In *The White Devil* (1612), Flamineo is a character with a very wide range. Even more spectacularly, Bosola in *The Duchess of Malfi* (1614) dominates the play. He is philosophical and sardonic, a wonderful player of roles, and his wild imagination seems to derive from Shakespearean characters like Richard, Duke of Gloucester and Iago.

NOTES

1. This point is well made by A. C. Bradley in discussing Iago as an artist: "His action is a plot, the intricate plot of a drama, and in the conception and the execution of it, he experiences the tension and the joy of artistic creation. . . . Here at any rate Shakespeare put a good deal of himself into Iago" (pp. 230–31). A. C. Bradley, *Shakespearean Tragedy*, London, 1950. First published 1904.

2. See Maurice Charney, *Style in Hamlet*. Princeton, NJ: Princeton University Press, 1969.

Bibliography

Alfar, Christina León. *Fantasies of Female Evil: The Dynamics of Gender and Power in Shakespearean Tragedy.* Newark, DE: University of Delaware Press, 2003.

Armstrong, Edward A. *Shakespeare's Imagination*, rev. ed. Lincoln, NE: University of Nebraska Press, 1963.

Barnet, Sylvan. "Coleridge on Shakespeare's Villains," *Shakespeare Quarterly*, 7 (1956), 9–20.

Bethell, S. L. "Shakespeare's Imagery: The Diabolic Images in *Othello*," *Shakespeare Survey*, 5 (1952), 62–80.

Bradley, A. C. *Shakespearean Tragedy.* London, UK: Macmillan, 1950. First published 1904.

Braunmuller, A. R. "Early Shakespearian Tragedy," in *Shakespearian Tragedy*, ed. David J. Palmer. New York, 1984, 96–128.

Brown, John Russell. Arden edition of *The Merchant of Venice.* London, UK: Methuen, 1955.

Charney, Maurice. *Style in Hamlet.* Princeton, NJ: Princeton University Press, 1969.

———. *Hamlet's Fictions.* New York, NY: Routledge, 1988.

———. *Titus Andronicus*, Harvester New Critical Introductions to Shakespeare. New York, NY: Harvester Wheatsheaf, 1990.

———. "Shylock as Villain," *Shakespeare Newsletter*, 59 (2009–2010), 85–86, 88, 100.

Clemen, Wolfgang, *A Commentary on Shakespeare's Richard III*, tr. Jean Bonheim. London, UK: 1968. First published 1957.

———. *The Development of Shakespeare's Imagery.* Cambridge, MA: Harvard University Press, 1951.

Coe, Charles Norton, *Shakespeare's Villains.* New York, NY: Bookman Associates, 1957.

———. *Demi-Devils: The Character of Shakespeare's Villains.* New York, NY: 1962.

Coleridge, Samuel Taylor. *Shakespearean Criticism*, 2 vols., ed. Thomas Middleton Raysor. London, UK: 1960.

Dachslager, Earl. "*'The Stock of Barabbas'*: Shakespeare's Unfaithful Villains," *Upstart Crow*, 6 (1986), 8–21.

Daniell, David. Arden edition of *Julius Caesar*. London, UK: Thomson Learning, 1988.

Eliot, T. S. "Christopher Marlowe," *Selected Essays 1917–1932*. New York, NY: 1932.

Empson, William."Honest in *Othello,*" in *The Structure of Complex Words*. London, UK: 1951.

Evans, Bertrand. *Shakespeare's Comedies*. London, UK: Oxford University Press, 1960.

Foakes, R. A. Arden edition of *King Lear*. London, UK: Thomson Learning, 1997.

Gibbons, Brian. Arden edition of *Romeo and Juliet*. London, UK: Methuen, 1980.

Goth, Maik. *From Chaucer's Pardoner to Shakespeare's Iago*. Frankfurt: Peter Lang, 2009.

Hammond, Anthony. Arden edition of *Richard III*. London, UK, Methuen, 1981.

Heilman, Robert Bechtold, *This Great Stage: Image and Structure in King Lear*. Baton Rouge, LA: Louisiana State University Press, 1948.

———. *Magic in the Web: Action and Language in Othello*. Lexington, KY: University of Kentucky Press, 1956.

Honigmann, E. A. J. Arden edition of *Othello*. London: Thomas Nelson, 1997.

———,. *Shakespeare: Seven Tragedies: The Dramatist's Manipulation of Response*. 2 ed., London, UK: 2002.

Hyman, Stanley Edgar. "Untuning the Othello Music: Iago as Stage Villain," in *The Rarer Action: Essays in Honor of Francis Fergusson*, ed. Alan Cheuse and Richard Koffler. New Brunswick, NJ: Rutgers University Press, 1970, 55–67.

Kaul, R. K. "Shakespeare's Portrayal of Evil," *Literary Criterion*, 11 (1974), 53–67.

Kliman, Bernice W., and Laury Magnus, eds. New Kittredge edition of *Romeo and Juliet*. Newburyport, MA: Focus Publishing, 2008.

Kreider, Paul V. *Repetition in Shakespeare's Plays*. Princeton, NJ: Princeton University Press, 1941.

Langbaum, Robert. "Character Versus Action in Shakespeare," *Shakespeare Quarterly*, 8 (1957), 57–69.

Leech, Clifford. "The Invulnerability of Evil," in *Shakespeare's Art: Seven Essays*, ed. Milton Crane. Chicago, IL: University of Chicago Press, 1973, 151–68.

Maguin, Jean-Marie. "Rise and Fall of the King of Darkness," in *French Essays on Shakespeare and His Contemporaries*, ed. Jean-Marie Maguin. Newark, DE: University of Delaware Press, 1995, 247–70.

Maxwell, J. C. Arden edition of *Titus Andronicus*. London, UK: Methuen, 1961.

McAlindon, Tom. "The Evil of Play and the Play of Evil: Richard, Iago and Edmund Contextualized," in *Shakespeare's Universe: Essays in Honour of W. R. Elton*. London, UK: Scolar Press, 1996, 148–54.

McEachern, Claire, Arden edition of *Much Ado About Nothing*. London, UK: Thomson Learning, 2006.

Muir, Kenneth. "Image and Symbol in 'Macbeth,'" *Shakespeare Survey,* 19 (1966), 45–54.

Ornstein, Robert. *A Kingdom for a Stage: The Achievement of Shakespeare's History Plays.* Cambridge, MA: Harvard University Press, 1972.

Pechter, Edward. *Othello and Interpretive Traditions.* Iowa City, IA: Iowa University Press, 1999.

Reibetanz, John. "The Cause of Thunder," *Modern Language Quarterly,* 46 (1985), 181–90.

Rosenberg, Marvin. "In Defense of Iago," *Shakespeare Quarterly,* 6 (1955), 45–58.

———. *The Masks of Othello.* Berkeley, CA: University of California Press, 1961.

———. *The Masks of King Lear.* Berkeley, CA: University of California Press, 1972.

Shapiro, James. *Shakespeare and the Jews.* New York, NY: Columbia University Press, 1996.

Smith, Molly. *The Darker World Within: Evil in the Tragedies of Shakespeare and His Successors.* Newark, DE: University of Delaware Press, 1991.

Snyder, Susan. *The Comic Matrix of Shakespeare's Tragedies.* Princeton, NJ: Princeton University Press, 1979.

Spevack, Bernard. *Shakespeare and the Allegory of Evil.* New York, NY: Columbia University Press, 1958.

Spivack, Charlotte. *The Comedy of Evil on Shakespeare's Stage.* Madison, NJ: Fairleigh Dickinson University Press, 1978.

Spurgeon, Caroline F. E. *Shakespeare's Imagery and What It Tells Us.* New York, NY: 1935.

Stephenson, A. A. "The Significance of *Cymbeline*," *Scrutiny,* 10 (1942), 329–38.

Stoll, Elmer E. "Heroes and Villains," *Review of English Studies,* 18 (1942), 257–69.

Ure, Peter. "Character and Role from *Richard III* to *Hamlet,*" in *Elizabethan and Jacobean Drama,* ed. J. C. Maxwell. Liverpool, UK: Liverpool University Press, 1974, Chapter 2.

Van Laan, Thomas F. *Role-playing in Shakespeare.* Toronto, ON: University of Toronto Press, 1978.

Washington, Edward T. "Vanishing Villains: The Role of Tarquin in Shakespeare's *Lucrece*," *Upstart Crow,* 14 (1994), 126–38.

Index

19136869R00104

Printed in Great Britain
by Amazon